D0674098

Leyla Aliyeva

The World Dissolves, like a Dream

Azerbaijan Translation Centre
London – 2018

Published in United Kingdom
Hertfordshire Press Ltd © 2018
9 Cherry Bank, Chapel Street
Hemel Hempstead, Herts.
HP2 5DE, United Kingdom

e-mail: publisher@hertfordshirepress.com
www.hertfordshirepress.com

Azerbaijan Translation Centre
The World Dissolves, like a Dream
English

Translated by **Anne Marie Jackson, Caroline Walton**
Edited by **Caroline Walton**
Designed by Agil Amrahov

British Library Catalogue in Publication DataA catalogue record for this book is available from the British Library Library of Congress in Publication DataA catalogue record for this book has been requested

ISBN 978-1-910886-76-2

Contents

Above the Clouds

This collection of poetry is the first book in Azerbaijani written by the talented young poet Leyla Aliyeva, who is known in our literary circles for moving poems, such as "Don't Go, Mother", "I will Go and Cry a Little", "The Swan", "The Butterfly", "To Each Their Own End" and "I am Blind". From her very first work, these poems have shown her own way of thinking and distinctive view of the world. They are like unfading flowers that retain sorrow, love, the warmth of the air, rain, drizzle and scent. For several years now Leyla Aliyeva has been earning the admiration of a wide, intellectual readership.

This book can be called a creative map on which the poet journeys over green, sunlit plains or along serpentine paths through precipices beset by thunder and lightning. As we draw closer, we can see the alienation of the innocent Angel who has come down to earth from above the clouds. We see her life in a foreign land, its meaning, its purpose. She is worn out from "truths" that cannot be grasped, her soul worn thin. She has escaped the narrowness of this world, the constricting frame, and now looks up to the unfamiliar expanses, now looks down with an unexpected thirst for life - we realize that these were the flights of the angel to Earth...

Spittle on the soul,
More spittle.
My heart sank
Between broken lines.

My heart sank,
Burdens grew heavier.
God, where do I go?
God, tell me, take pity me.

Could there be a moment
More powerful than days or months?
Perhaps - and, unfortunately,
Time is irreversible.

Why was the laughter suddenly louder?
What is hiding true smiles?
There's nothing more sensitive
Than this soul of mine.

Beneath the skin it lies torn,
Beneath the skin, which thickened.
That which costs the most,
Is lost easily, as though cast to the seas.

It sinks. I don't dare
Throw it a lifebuoy,
I really want to and I try -
But my hands have no strength.

I can't raise my wrists,
A glance of frozen pain.
The tale is erased from the book,
It can't be recovered.

They erased my favourite tale,
I want to shout: "Don't!"
Only there's no strength in my voice,
My lips burn with an aftertaste of poison.

What changed suddenly?
Winter has come.

But in fact it's been chilly for a long time,
I just didn't notice.

The leaves fell from the trees,
Twilight descends in the afternoon.
How can I not believe in this?
How can I not know this?

The author has the outstanding ability to put down on paper all that happens in God's wide world - pain and weariness, love and sorrow, joy and tears, while retaining the atmosphere of the very moment itself, reliving it with all the strength of its impact. These verses contain an incomprehensible, life-giving energy. Here, grief, sorrow, loneliness and hopelessness are as compassionate and invigorating as love, joy, surprise and admiration of the world's divine beauty, which is hidden from a simple gaze. But most important is the victory of truth and love over the world, over people's invented, unsustainable, illogical "logic".

* * *

The Angel is eager to understand the hidden truths of the world. But she is alone on Earth; in this endless stream of people, she has no-one but the dark, still nights, the wind, the clouds, the Sun and Moon. Neither moonlit nights nor weeping rains, neither wild winds nor days, neither months nor seasons melted in the mirage of thoughts and senses can help... Friends, familiar faces... visions stripped of support, foundation, absolute truth... The flickering of mutually contradictory, pitiless mirages...

The Angel is alone in this chaotic world. But she never gives up – like a moth lost in the dark of night, she doesn't tire of striking the windows through which the light glimmers.

This is how the Angel lives. In the hope of saving the world through love from its manifold ills and sufferings, by fighting the essence of darkness and unfathomable mystery, spreading the delicate dust of his wings to all four corners and losing it, wearing herself out among unanswered questions...

Unable to understand consciousness and thought, living in some untouchable heights, this pain, this weariness is not a human kind of weariness and pain; resembling rain, floods, earthquakes, occasionally the familiar, hopeless stillness of solitary, mute nights, this is a very different pain, a different weariness. It is impossible to leave this world, filled with divine love and mercy, to move quietly away from it, without getting wet and cold and shivering.

It's the inimitable, boundless love, carried like a torch in the Angel's heart, that does not let her give up and turn into a human... It is Divine Love that fills her wings and soul with clouds, sunlight, and rain and brings healing to humankind.

The Angel has come to the world with this mission – to give to humankind this Love obtained from the Sun, rain and clouds, which it has long forgotten, and rescue humankind from the dead abyss it has rolled into.

The Angel herself is unaware of this. Though she is able to hold in the palm of her hand the whole world – people, trees, the sea, the Sun and Moon in the Light of boundless Love, the only refuge for the Angel in Heaven and on Earth is her own Soul.

And where did time fly so quickly,
Outside it's already winter again!
I think I've become ill with ennui,
Yes, the soul of summer has caught cold!
Roses don't bloom under the sun in the garden,
The Caspian sand doesn't sparkle!
Icy grief burns the chests

Of those who're forever alone.
Why are you cold, my heart?
How can I melt your ice?
But you don't want to get warm,
Your soul mourns with winter!
And where did time fly so quickly?
I shouted to it: "Wait!"
At six o'clock the road darkened,
In vain I stretched out my hand to the sun!
If I could reach it,
I would hide it in my hands!
And then the night would not come,
Night is witness to tears!
Forgive me, my heart,
I won't hurt you anymore!
Nowhere can I escape from you,
And no way can you understand me!

The Angel is here, but she does not know why she has come to Earth. She knows one thing for sure – she is invincible. Like the Sun itself. Like the winds, the rains and claps of thunder.

Over time, the Angel, whose heart is filled with love and mercy, will strike many windows, enter the forbidden darkness, throw open the hidden doors to Salvation, and explain to Humankind who she is. And then ... caught up in the clouds and winds, she will return from whence she came.

The delicate dust of her wings will remain on the window panes. Sun, Rain, Thunder and Wind will not touch these tiny particles of dust. These delicate particles will shine for long years and centuries to come; shedding light all around, they will continue to talk to people.

Afag Masud
Writer

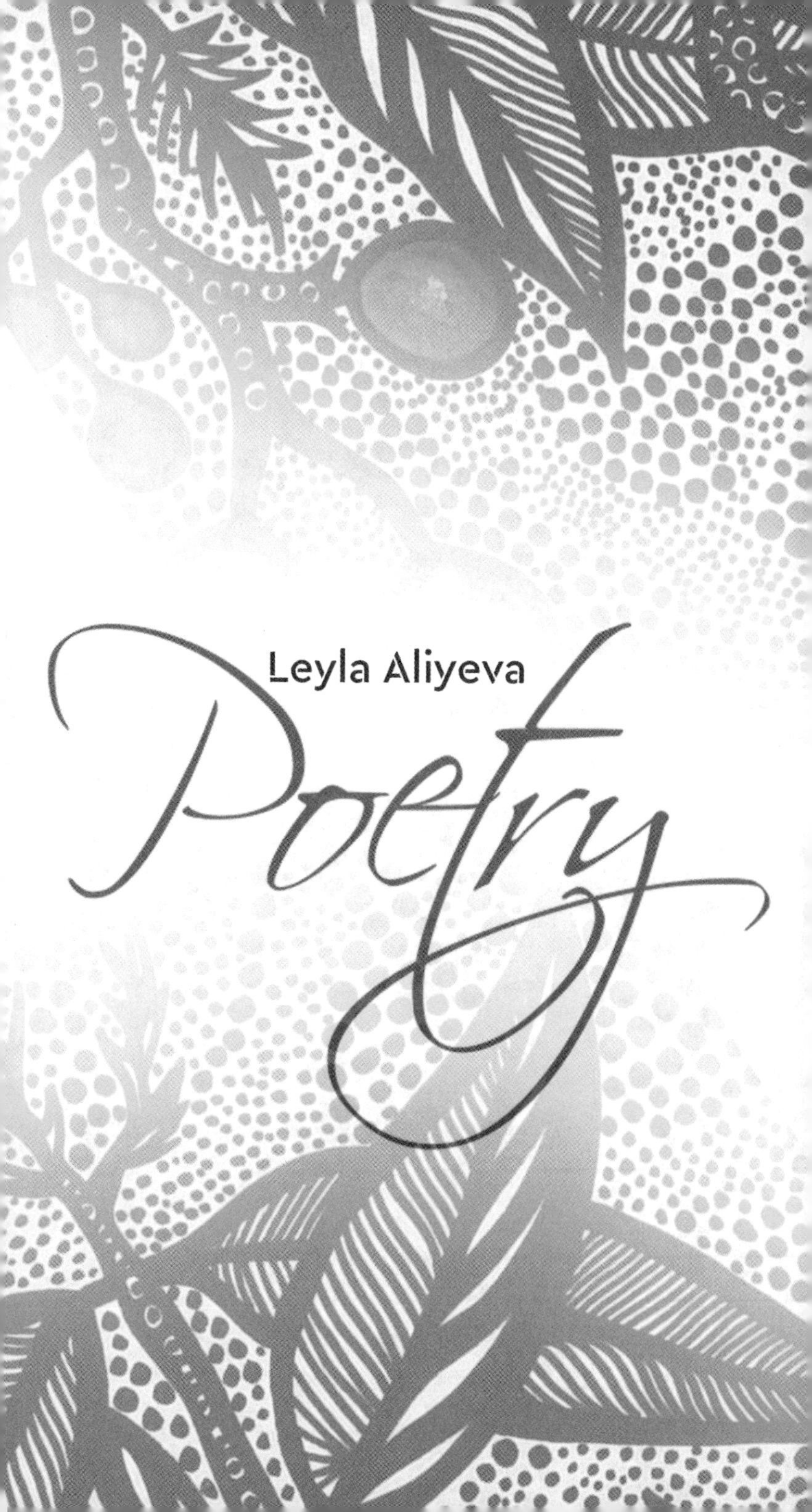
Leyla Aliyeva
Poetry

The World Dissolves, like a Dream

O my friend so sweet and loving

O my friend so sweet and loving
Why do you endlessly weep?
Love, like life, is not eternal.
It can break the fragile heart.

Look around you – so many people
Rushing down the road to nowhere
But I came into this world on my own,
And when I die I'll leave alone.

Swallow your pride; soar - don't fall,
Don't submit to worldly vanity.
For the strongest is also weak
When his soul meets adversity.

My friend, you think you know so much
And yet you know so little.
A single road shows what is right,
A road for all... a road for none.

Tell me, my friend, where are you rushing?
To whom do you seek to cling?
It might just be easier to release
That which you fear to set free.

As for me, I seek repentance,
For sins that cause such torment
For us perhaps there's no defence,
But I should not pass judgement.

I'll go and shed a few tears

I'll go and shed a few tears.
Just like that; only a few!
I'll hide my heart beneath a pillow.
Toss it through an open window.
I'll go and shed a few tears,
I won't say how unhappy I am.
I'll take my heart to the dacha
Where I'll leave it to drown in the sea.
I'll cast my heart to the wind
And let it be carried away.
My heart has not the words to say
Why it must cause me such pain.
I'll bury it here in the flower bed
So it can bloom in blue and red.
Then I'll smear it with sweet honey
To hide its bitter emptiness.
I'll ask some guests over to dine;
We'll make ourselves drunk on wine.

Then I'll serve my heart on a platter,
And let them eat their fill.
Those children playing outside,
Perhaps they'd like a football?
Come here and take my heart!
We're finished with sorrow now!
I'll flog it on the market,
You can have it for nothing!
It contains barbs that sting
And a pitiless volcano!
In the sad nocturnal silence
We two are left together.
When it rains I'll hide the brolly
And leave my heart out to soak.
'Come and take it forever'
I'll wail to the sun and the moon!
Why, oh why did I not decide
To make it a gift to you?

Mama, please don't leave me!

Mama, please don't leave me!
Mama, please don't go!
When you're not here, Mama,
The rain never ends.

Take me in your arms,
Press me to your heart,
Ignite the stars in the sky
With a spark from your magic eyes.

Mama, I'm only small,
I cannot utter words,
I've yet to read books,
I dare not judge the world.

Mama, I'm only small,
Scarcely able to walk.
I don't yet know life;
I want to know you.

Mama, please, tell me why
You weep from time to time.
And why is it, when I'm grown
I'll hear so many lies?

I'll play with my dolls
The way adults play at life.
I'll learn to hold my tongue
For adults are full of secrets.

I'll learn to be afraid, sad,
Anxious and unhappy.
It's a pity I'll stop believing
That anything can happen.

I'm sorry I must say goodbye
To all my childish dreams.
Of course, in sleep at night,
Mama will come to me.

I won't build castles –
I've so little time and strength
But when I'm grown I'll be sorry
And decide to start over again.

But when I'm grown I'll repent,
Recalling childhood tales.
Only then will I recognise
My true heart's desire.

Mama, believe me,
If only I could speak,
You would learn the way to live
In this world, from a child's lips.

Mama, please don't leave me!
Mama, come back, I beg you!
Mama, believe me when I say
That what I breathe is you!

We run, we fly away

We run, we fly away,
We're so afraid; we thirst for love!
We launch ships on the oceans
To carry us far out to sea!

We run, we fly away,
Splutter of engine, hoot of car,
We divert the mind's eye from the heart
For the heart travels better when light.

Planes soar like birds in flight
Only birds don't hurry.
In our rush we've ceased to dream,
Our mind's eye no longer sees!

I scrawl these lines,
I've five minutes I'm told,
I'm forgetting to put in the stops,
Yet those who need to will understand!

I scrawl these lines
I've poems, like balsam, in my heart.
Tailbacks are making me late
But my poems won't be marred by fate!

Goodbye, my friend, goodbye,
I truly don't care for farewells.
But now I have memoirs,
And someday I may read them!

I'll recall a day long forgotten,
Like the wind the years will fly by!
I'll remember how I hurried in vain,
And ask "What for?" and "Why?"

I don't yet have an answer,
Nor a minute to solve the secret of life.
What am I closing my eyes to?
Excuse me, please, I must run...

Shops, restaurants...

Shops, restaurants...
I'm in such pain,
That I switch off the light -
In the darkness wounds can't be seen,
If they're invisible,
It means they're not there.

Bus stop, waiting...
I'm waiting for a red bus,
The one that won't come.
The precious recognition
That awaits
Those who dare be foolish.

A sea of noise,
Yet how quiet it is...
No words left to say.
Whoever created the world
Never imagined how shallowly
We would live in it.

Bus stop, where's the bus?
Nothing here but black cabs.
Not what I need.
And what if there was?
If there was a bus
But no taxis.

So much light!
It's Christmas after all.
We shall celebrate merrily.
Without secrets or pretence,
Pretending with a prick of conscience,
We shall wait.

Shops, restaurants...
New Year's lights strung everywhere.
How hollow it is,
And a little bit strange
How they've forgotten to hang lights
On our souls.

Time

Time, would you stop please?
Please wait and take me with you.
Let me know where you're running to.
I'll share my own secrets in return.

I want to discover your long journey.
Time, after all, fears no one.
Hurtling over all and everyone,
Never saying where it's headed.

Tell me, I beg you, just what
In this world is so irreplaceable
That it costs your peace of mind?
Why does your soul burn so?

Perhaps I don't understand much,
Perhaps I understand too much.
I have it all; I'm losing everything in my soul.
Everything surrounds me, how is it I'm all
alone?

I half-open my eyes for a moment,
And pity what is around me,
Realising I am pitiful too.
I close my eyes again, for good.

Recognising how fine everything is,
Like a hair, so difficult to tear,
I'll hide my face behind the mask,
Of life, and smile forever.

Time, I ask you, don't forget
This moment, this balcony, this ship, this sea,
Time, don't leave me behind,
I beg you, take me with you.

Tears

I wanted to cry but had no tears,
Tell me whose fault is that?
The frost froze my tears like icicles,
It's so nice to share poems with a poet!

I wanted to cry, not knowing why
I didn't cry – I lost the will!
Let me tell you, crying is healthy,
And for some, it may come easily!

Tell me, what is life now,
What lurks in my future?
Sometimes I see what lies ahead,
Without ever regretting a thing!

The emptiness of dark eyes fatigued me
As the desert wilts in the heat.
Perhaps I held my tongue in vain,
Perhaps in vain. Who knows?

There's silence without and silence within,
It's there, it's always around.
It's suddenly settled within my heart,
I haven't a thing to fear!

'Wait!' they'll tell me, 'Don't rush!
At least think it over a little!'
Forgive me, reason, I don't know how to wait,
To me, 'Think it over' means 'Think twice.'

But I don't want to think twice,
My whole body and soul refuse!
Don't waste your breath, don't ask, my dears!
For my dreams will tell me everything!

January has come and rapped at the door,
How very quickly he's appeared!
He promised to pay us a visit!
The grass grows cold; even the rain has passed,
"I'll soon be back!" he said.

He's back and he's happy,
Says it's a year since we met.
Although it seems only half an hour
Since January and I parted on the threshold.

I sit here alone. Yes, alone, and so what?
Is being alone such a crime?
Perhaps it is; it doesn't matter.
May time punish me for my sins.

We may be criminals; we may be heroes
But we'll never be angels.
Yet there is an angel beside me; he comes often,
And no one will ever deceive him.

Goodbye, friends! I must go now.
You can be sure I'll be back soon!
Everyone's going, we only need permission
Everyone returns! Don't regret a thing!

Goodbye, my friends!
How I hate to say goodbye!
In the receding silence I'll say:
"Till we meet again, farewell!"

Slave of Love

There lived a Slave of Love, wandering the desert
In search of water in dried-up ponds.
Snared like a victim in a spider's web,
He cursed the angels in heaven!

High on a mountain lived the Master of Love,
The whole world spread before his eyes!
With a dour and hollowed spirit
He cursed the angels in a rage!

At night beneath a shooting star,
Caught up in an impossible dream,
With the desire of fever, the indignity of poison,
The Slave listened for the voice of unattainable love!

And the Master sat beneath the burning sun
With a pile of wounded hearts!
Reading books a hundred times over
Whose tiresome endings he knew by heart!

The Slave wept bitterly, felt such hatred,
Conceived a million tender things to say!
He was struck blind, and in the darkness
could only see
The distant sparkle of his beloved's eyes!

And the Master drank wine without pleasure,
Forgetting the one who waited with such ardour,
Killing time out of boredom,
He gets away with murder!

A clap of thunder resounded
In the Slave's delirious heart,
And puddles looked like an ocean
While the Slave died to life, he lived on in dreams!

But the dreams of the Master were barren,
Mere glimpses of bare woods!
He did not seek love long forgotten,
And no longer believed in miracles!

Tell me which of the two is happier?
Hard to say who is Master and who is Slave!
Alas, this question has no answer!
Better to love or be loved, who can say?

Letter

I never once wrote to you,
I feared to, for I knew
That I couldn't find the words to tell you
What I held so deep in my heart.

Alas, the dictionary lacks words
To convey my feelings,
I therefore kept quiet,
Wishing to say everything through silence.

You hear everything, you understand everything,
You see the rain, even in cloudless skies,
You read eyes like a book,
As the sun bestows its rays.

You will feel a cold wind,
What is hiding behind the stone wall?
Let all the world's ships take offence,
As they crash into an iceberg.

Let every candle melt in the dark,
There are stars to illuminate our path,
It's night again; I wait for you in dreams,
For the sake of meeting you I could sleep forever!

Night again! And now truth appears,
Mirrors no longer deceive,
Night again! I'm not alone in it!
For you are near, even if I'm alone!

Go, cross the peaks,
Swim all the rivers, all the seas,
Walk through endless valleys,
For you know I am waiting for you.

Don't cry. Is there any reason?
Don't ask me to be yours forever,
I cannot live just as one half,
Is it possible to grasp eternity?

I never once wrote to you,
But I decided to write all the same,
Alas, the dictionary lacks words,
Except these: I love!

Lie

Lie, we promise never to lie,
What are we ashamed to tell, and to whom?
Lies, they poison our hearts
Those who don't speak the truth, fear it.

You shouldn't believe that lies
Will bring smiles and light to darkness,
And who said that it's stupid to grieve?
Don't hide what is sincere.

Grieve if you want to or have fun,
If you're guilty, pray to God,
For everyone knows what they've done,
The sunset won't hide the truth.

You deceived, but won no victory,
Whoever spoke the truth, won?
Take pity on him, help him,
The treacherous night won't let him sleep.

Lies, there are plenty of excuses,
Life has become like an old film.
Take a chance and promise not to lie,
It's not worth selling your freedom to the devil.

Take a risk, friend, you won't regret it,
Walk in the rain without an umbrella.
Whoever speaks the truth has nothing to fear,
You can't escape from the truth.

Whom did you deceive, though you know quite well?
Now you'll answer for everything,
And even though no one knows or understands,
The mind is dogged by eternal fear.

But conscience quietly corrodes the mind,
Time slowly melts into remorse,
You lied, even if everyone believes you,
You didn't deceive yourself by lying to yourself!

I'm leaving

I'm leaving, you know this,
It's no use hoping for a miracle,
I shall never belong
To anyone.

I'm leaving; don't cry,
Only fools cry,
Don't waste feelings on me,
I can't live otherwise.

They say that every person
Has another half.
I don't want to know about that,
Solitude is dear to me.

They say that God created
All living things as pairs,
But I don't believe these words.
For each of us is alone,

I'm leaving, don't beg,
Don't ask me to stay,
Don't be sad, don't grieve.
I know, I'll remember.

I'm leaving. Why then,
You ask, did I give so much?
Everything ends; it's a shame
That beginnings have so little value.

It's a pity that so many stupid feelings
Evaporate somewhere.
My world has long been empty,
I'm leaving; I shan't return.

I'm leaving; you won't forgive me,
Calling me heartless
You won't release me from your heart.
I'm leaving; leaving for good.

Summer

May God let us live for 100 years,
And not 36,000 days,
It makes no sense to live for so few days,
Even if days fly by faster.

Today is worse than yesterday,
And forget about tomorrow,
What a dreary spring,
We're all fed up with winter.

But summer yes, let summer come!
Even if it's blazing hot,
Then cold will return, condemning us
To autumnal darkness.

Let's wait for tomorrow,
One day, maybe a year?
For he blamed the rain,
But the rain is not eternal; the rain will pass.

We have to wait a little,
In a week there'll be sun,
It will disappear again,
But they say it'll return in spring!

Spring, of course everyone loves spring,
Let it come again in March,
But I don't like February,
It will last for 29 days.

But 29 days are a trifle,
They will pass unnoticed,
We'll endure them somehow,
In the eternal expectation of summer!

Such hands, how skilled they are

Such hands, how skilled they are
With the eyes, they create uniqueness.
Those hands were not spared,
By the philistines who tried to condemn them.

You're a fool; you shouldn't have listened to them,
Your soul is much too fine for that.
You thought – why do we need ears?
And suddenly cut one off in a rage.

Alone at night you dreamed of recognition,
How many rights have those who recognise?
Alone you dreamed in sad expectation,
But we, alas, don't wait for those who wait!

He who creates beautiful things,
Who wants to create beauty,
Alas, so often doesn't spare himself,
Wishing to destroy, on account of that talent.

Tell me, why do you try to justify yourself?
Why did you cry so bitterly in the silence?
You did not win great recognition,
What your dreams recognised was greater.

You thought that your flowers would wither,
But you went on creating them in the dark,
Canvasses are not people; they can't deceive,
Your flowers will live forever.

Love and hate

Love, why are such friends with hatred?
It weakens you, wounds you.
Love, you need no one except love.
Don't be afraid - he who loves will conquer.

Go; don't be mired in resentment,
Close your eyes so that jealousy can't blind you.
But even if your eyes stay open,
Don't forget for a moment to love.

Love, you're stupid if you believe
That pride will protect you like a stone wall,
Tell me, for whom do you play games?
Surely you play for yourself.

Love, why are you so afraid of love?
It can never be unhappy,
As long as you never say goodbye to hope,
As long as you never stop loving.

Love, you don't want to be rejected?
And what does that mean, do you know?
After all, day always ends in night,
And night is when dreams begin.

Don't cry love, I beg you, please, don't,
Sometimes I too cry at night.
No, I don't need the moon and the stars,
But I won't give up the love in my heart.

Love, why are you such friends with hatred?
You can't take possession of me, hate.
Love, you make my head swirl so much,
That I couldn't bear to live without you!

People

People! How difficult it is always to love you,
How easy it is sometimes to hate you!
People, try to make each other happy!
People, try not to hurt each other!

People walk, run, hurry into the distance,
While clinging to past moments.
Smiles, tears, groans, blood and sweat!
Their breath doesn't even notice the passage of time!

They don't notice their own joy or sadness,
They fly along selfishly, without conscience!
For time, human vanity is nothing.
We cannot comprehend time's expanse.

Time, you know, I envy you!
I love you; I'm jealous and madly passionate!
Be only mine both in the morning and in dreams,
I want to shackle you in chains!

Time, you can belong to me forever!
After all, I'm different, you know!
I'd give you everything to hold on to you!
Burning all, in my hands you melt!

I weep, but my eyes shed no tears!
If tears were forever forbidden,
How priceless would each one be,
Caught behind eyelashes, hidden.

People! Do not kill each other senselessly.
Life will do that brutal job for you!
Care for each other selflessly,
Even the mighty seas will appreciate that!

Night, I feel you so passionately!
Night, you gave me stars in the sky,
I won't share you; I won't lose you!
With you I forget my loneliness!

Well, let us forgive each other
For eternal grievances, and grow a little stronger.
I see so much when my eyes are closed,
People! Please try to love each other!

I do not believe

Spittle on the soul,
More spittle.
My heart sank
Between broken lines.

My heart sank,
Burdens grew heavier.
God, where do I go?
God, tell me, take pity me.

Could there be a moment
More powerful than days or months?
Perhaps - and, unfortunately,
Time is irreversible.

Why was the laughter suddenly louder?
What is hiding true smiles?
There's nothing more sensitive
Than this soul of mine.

Beneath the skin it lies torn,
Beneath the skin, which thickened.
That which costs the most,
Is lost easily, as though cast to the seas.

It sinks. I don't dare
Throw it a lifebuoy,
I really want to and I try -
But my hands have no strength.

I can't raise my wrists,
A glance of frozen pain.
The tale is erased from the book,
It can't be recovered.

They erased my favourite tale,
I want to shout: "Don't!"
Only there's no strength in my voice,
My lips burn with an aftertaste of poison.

What changed suddenly?
Winter has come.
But in fact it's been chilly for a long time,
I just didn't notice.

The leaves fell from the trees,
Twilight descends in the afternoon.
How can I not believe in this?
How can I not know this?

Night

Night, forgive me, but I don't like you.
Not because I consider myself more beautiful -
But only in the dark I see
The false secrets I kept in the day.

Night, forgive me, but you're not my friend,
Although friends will only tell the truth,
But in truth, alas, lies a sea of torment,
While day veneers artifice over pain.

Night, tell me why you came,
Reminding me of all that is forgotten,
Cruelly invoking dreams,
Dreams that sunlight hides?

Night, believe me, you reveal yourself in vain,
Only fairy tales can be so sincere,
Whether a man is a genius or a fool,
By day he hides his self behind a mask.

Night, give up your false sense of peace,
Dawn's rays soothe like balsam,
Return smiles and hide anxiety -
Anxiety that only your fog reveals.

Night, don't cry and don't pity me,
For if you want, we'll cry together,
You are merciful, but try as you will,
You cannot hold back time.

Night, tell me, you like everyone, will leave,
You go, leaving me to the gloom of day,
Which means, like everyone else, you also lie,
Giving hope, but not healing the soul.

I do not want to leave you

I do not want to leave you,
I can't do otherwise.
"Why play - to lose?"
Your cruel mind asks you.

Why did you play? And you lost,
You knew, sooner or later.
Of course you knew, but played all the same,
Not seriously believing in victory.

In this there is no victory,
There couldn't be.
Forgive me, but life is not a movie,
So what's bothering you now?

What do your eyes express -
The doubt of a young man's heart?
But still you waited and believed in vain
For us the end is quite different.

There can be no other ending.
But in the end is a beginning,
I know it's hard to lose.
I know – I lost myself.

I want to say to you: "Forgive me!"
But will this make it easier?
And ask that you let go of all
That, in losing, you clasp more tightly.

I want to tell you: "Don't cry!" -
You're not one to cry.
I want to tell you: "Forget me!"
But you're not one to forget.

I want to ask you not to give me
That sad and greedy look.
You did not have me near you,
Even when I was by your side.

Although, of course, you once had
My mind – but not for long,
You didn't fall head over heels -
I confess, I'm to blame.

I sense my guilt,
But tell me, what will change this?
I won't live with guilt all my life,
It will vanish before dawn.

And with it you will disappear,
Therefore, please don't
Descend to worldly vanity,
Hold onto the light of the fading sun.

I cannot be with you,
But "I cannot" does not exist.
I'll go on living without you,
That's all that troubles me.

And don't cut down the forest,
That sprang up between us.
Leaving so cruelly,
I'll abandon faith with every step.

Another page of disappointment

Another page of disappointment
Added to the notebook of my soul,
Without full stops or commas; without despair,
I wrote down what I knew to expect.

Everything is predictable to the point of
absurdity,
Life has become like a stupid movie,
Replaying it a hundred times, still believing
in miracles,
The plot won't change anyway.

Probably hopes are the last to die,
Clinging to the mind until the last breath,
Although you know everything will remain
as before,
The mind won't let go of the shadow
of anticipation.

Openly deceiving themselves,
People have got used to existing on earth,
Only seeing what we see, not noticing
the universe,
Why would we, the unseeing, notice it?

We're so contemptuous of the animal herd,
They're inferior; we can't tell them apart,
We don't consider ourselves a herd,
Yet what's the difference? We merged long ago.

Probably there's no other way,
Homo sapiens wouldn't survive in the world,
To perceive reality is so difficult,
My eyes water, trying to peer more closely.

My eyes were blinded; my heart rusted over,
I swear, at times, I don't want to live,
But I skilfully hide pain and despair,
Like everyone else, I'm not worthy to judge others.

Don't go away

Don't go, please wait,
Don't leave me alone,
Stay with me a little longer,
I'm crazy with loneliness.

Don't flatter me with bold words,
They only make the deception more painful,
I made enemies out of friends,
To be a closer friend to you.

Don't exchange me for evil,
You see, I'm not like anyone else.
I hate the world, because
People live in it like the dead.

I curse everyone around,
For their sweetness, for their pretence,
For the stupid cunning with which they lie,
Believing in their own superiority.

Don't betray me to others,
Believe me, they aren't worth it,
I'll give my life to strangers,
If I don't share it with you.

Don't become like everyone else,
For they're weak and petty,
Like slaves, they follow fate,
Living lives of pretence.

Don't forget me, wherever you are,
But if I suddenly slip your mind,
Then, when you remember again,
Don't be angry because you miss me.

I'm not seeking casual meetings,
They only make the heart ache more,
What's precious is hard to preserve,
And only takes a moment to lose.

Don't go, don't leave me
In the desert of darkness without light,
I didn't have time to say goodbye,
I'll know you're no longer by my side.

I'll punish myself for that

I'll punish myself,
For behaving badly yesterday,
For those whom I cruelly offended,
For the copious wine I drank,
To drown my conscience more quickly.

I'll punish myself for loud laughter,
For the truth of words I spoke in vain,
I'll punish myself for my beauty,
For the fact that the world lay at my feet.

Sometimes I long to be myself,
Though I don't know who I've become,
The devil holds power over my soul,
I'm tired of goodness and angels.

So many sad and pitiful faces surround me,
The hungry devour me with their eyes,
I am the only friend I have,
To be my companion in joy and sorrow.

And I'll replace the pain that gnaws at my mind
In the dark, with one that destroys my body,
The heat of desire will cover solid ice,
So as not to lose everything that I never had.

Let everyone weep and live in sorrow,
My eyes will remain dry,
Smiles hide the pain that rends my heart
I'll leave my soul in the silence of the desert.

I'll punish myself, and after that,
I'll enjoy the torment of passion,
And vowing not suffer anymore,
I'll enjoy the suffering of others.

Elegy

If the stars were stairs,
And the moon lit up the track,
I would climb up to the sky,
And I would fetch you back.

If the wind could express,
All that grips my soul,
I'd shout out how I miss you,
So the world would know.

Your voice speaks in my heart,
The dearest sound I've heard,
If rivers could convey
An echo of your words!

If only the clouds could show me
How to find my way to you,
How I dream to hold your hand
For an instant, before you go.

If only the rain could tell me:
Why it fills the seas with tears.
If only the moon could tell me,
About the peace in your heart, my dear.

You're my defender from afar,
I sense your kindness; I've no fear
If the mountains could express,
How I love you, then you'd hear.

If that tree became a bridge,
I'd cross to you today,
And tell you with a smile
All the things I cannot say.

If night would turn to day,
And the sun light up the dark,
I would hug you tight,
We'd no longer be apart.

You were the best in the world,
I'll keep your memory, my love.
I'll wait for you forever,
I'll believe, and I will love.

Give me a word

Give me a word,
So I could say one in response.
Just one word,
I'll press it to my heart so as not to lose it.

Give me your hand,
I'll give you three hands back.
Don't be angry with ennui -
Without it, joy would bore us.

Look - at least once in a while,
I want you to look at me for a long time.
The cell door was opened, my soul
Flew out. Now it knows no limits.

Speak your grievances aloud -
If you don't you might do harm.
If we don't admit
How we torment each other, we shall drift apart.

Ask forgiveness,
It won't undermine your remorse.
Whoever doesn't realise this,
Will go on living among artificial shadows.

Give me much,
And I'll give you much in return,
But the one who is greedy,
Through ignorance, lets hours be stolen from him.
Don't be afraid of fear,
Even the bravest are afraid.
Do battle with it -
Overcoming it, you will become stronger.

Just be kind
And help those whose souls are in darkness;
Don't expect any return -
A kindness to others is a kindness to oneself.
Give me a word.
One of your favourites in a sea of words,
And I, unbeliever,
Will believe in transcendent love.

In Rome, on a dirty bench

In Rome, in November,
Quietly sitting on a dirty bench.
Next to a homeless man without a mask,
What's on his mind?

I smell alcohol,
Filth, cigarette smoke.
What have we in common?
I think he's tired of life.

Every passer-by stares at us
Bewilderment in their eyes.
But maybe we are similar?
His mouth is devoid of lies.

He has no reason to lie or deceive,
There's only an abyss in front of him,
There's nothing to find, nothing to lose,
No need to pretend.

He gently falls asleep on the bench,
Emitting a snore of despair.
Every person is given a dream,
Every one of us a living slave.

So in some ways we're similar -
That's the answer to the question.
Together, in Rome, beneath the eternal pines
The wind blew us away.

I'm not afraid of cruel nights

I'm not afraid of cruel nights,
I'm not afraid of biting winds.
I'll pass through the fates of people,
such lonely people,
I'll pass through and I won't return.
I'm not afraid of their tears of sorrow,
I'm not moved by a pathetic "stop".
I'll pass through, remaining in memories and stupid expectations,
I'll pass through like an iceberg.
I'm not afraid of eternal grievances,
Cocktails of love and hate,
With a treacherous and irreproachable glance,
I'll leave my steps behind me.
I'm not afraid that it will hurt,
Others don't care about my pain,
Let them wither like flowers, but wither
of their own accord,
Not forgiving me their whole life long.
I'm not afraid when the sun hides,
I'm not sad when it rains,
I'm leaving like time, and time won't turn back,
Oblivious to eternal cries of "wait!"
I'm not scared of fear,
I don't cry when my heart aches,
I'll give myself away - so cold and
so madly passionate,
I'll give away what belongs only to me.
I'm not afraid of giving myself away naively,

But I'm not ashamed to cunningly disappear,
I'm whole in myself – not someone's other half.
Alas, I can't hold back the winds.
I'm not afraid that I'm so afraid of being afraid,
Or that I'm insanely scared of being alone.
When everyone cries, I laugh and smile,
Alone, I'll cry beneath the moon.
I'm not afraid that I'm slowly losing my life,
It recedes farther every day,
Furling the umbrella, I wish and wish and wish,
I want to get wet in the rain.
I'm not afraid to believe in miracles,
I won't cease to believe in miracles,
The locks were smashed, opening all the doors
of my heart,
So that only emptiness remains.
I'm not afraid of cruel nights,
I'm not afraid of biting winds,
I'll pass through the fates of people,
such lonely people,
I'll pass through - and maybe I'll come back.

I had a dream...

I had a dream that fish
Could fly like birds!
You know how much
I miss you, and your words!

Snow falls outside,
Snow falls in my soul!
If you were close at hand,
I would have told you!

With one look,
You would have soothed my pain!
If I had you by my side,
The sun would shine again!

Like the shining sun,
Clouds cannot dim your light!
It seemed to us that you -
Will be forever bright!

They say time heals,
Well, I thank the hours!
But I won't give my memories
To adorn them; they're ours!

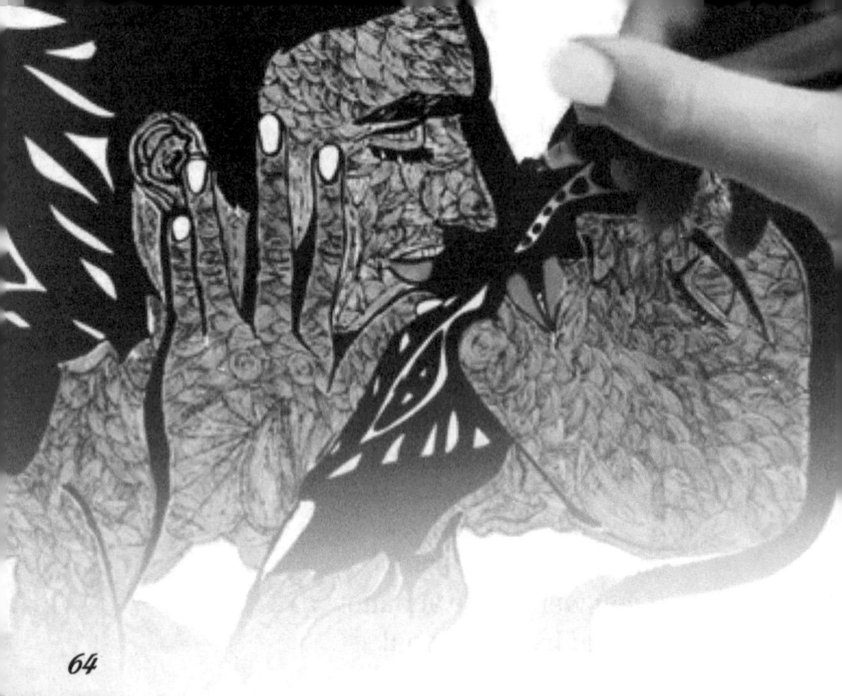

They say time heals,
Well, how you cured us!
We shall always feel the absence,
Of your warmth and tenderness!

Know that we'll always remember
Your humour and your smiles,
And we suddenly glimpsed Paradise,
Through your expressive eyes.

You have left the earth!
You live beyond it now!
Illuminating the dark night!
Brighter than the Plough!

Ego

Ego, you're taller than mountains, broader
than valleys!
Deeper than the ocean and louder
than the winds,
Are you angry for no reason?
You don't have the right words!

Ego, why so much outrage?
Did someone surpass you?
How cruelly doubts torment
The one so in love with himself!

Ego decided to be capricious again,
Spoiling everyone's mood.
What's the reason this time?
Who injured you and how?

Ego, you're in everyone's body,
But not everyone lets you reach the soul,
You tried to ascend to the sky,
In order to fall lower than the abyss!

Ego, we're all subject to you,
And the genius will become a fool.
Nothing is more dangerous than you,
You're such close friends with evil!

The ego blinds eyes with fog,
Gives lips bitter poison to drink!
Full of complexes and lies,
You drive people into eternal hellfire!

Ego ... Let's drive him out,
Even if he claims to be king!
Alas he has no crown, no throne,
And he looks just like a jester!

Can you stop loving me?

Can you stop loving me?
I asked you in silence.
After all, you won't die; you'll go on living,
I drink sweet tea to numb the pain.

Will you suffer for centuries?
Or forget me in a year and two
Will you erase my outline from the paper?
Or will you colour it in?

You can lose me,
And not look for the sun at sunset,
Don't stop, don't speak,
A spent word will not return.

Of course you can, everyone can,
Time hastily steals the breath away,
Losing me on this earth,
To keep the dream stronger.

You can forget me,
We forget everything sooner or later,
I taught you not to be sad,
I'm guilty for your sorrow.

I'm to blame all along,
But you'll forgive me, I know this,
Breaking fragile hearts,
I gather their shards into my own.

You can stop loving me,
Yes you can, I'll tell you a secret,
As long as I love myself
I will live in you forever!

But beauty has power

We don't believe drunks;
we don't believe children,
And only fools believe in fables!
But who can tell us,
Why at night we dream of miracles?

We don't believe those who see jinns,
Or someone who loves with all their heart.
We usually think they are liars,
We only value facts, not believing in dreams!

And how easy it is to offend a fool,
Who sincerely gives his heart!
From love, he will learn to hate,
He will die a slave to love.

We don't believe children,
we don't believe drunks,
Even if they speak the truth.
But beauty is treacherous,
She always forgives everyone and everything.

And beauty has power,
She's a sharp sword in battle!
She lures reason straight into the grave
With one flick of her shoulder!

We don't believe children;
we don't believe drunks!
We pay them no attention.
Those in the wrong always stick to their guns,
In order to hide their mistakes.

But beauty, alas, is not eternal!
Time washes colour from the canvas,
And the one who loves so deeply
Is freed from the agitation of words.

We don't believe children;
we don't believe drunks,
No masks hide their faces.
Wine wipes deceit from the lips.
How much truth the insolent speak!

And how to find the road to happiness?
There are so many traps on the way!
By not surrendering to the heat of passion,
It's easy to evade those snares.

We don't believe children;
we don't believe drunks,
At times we don't believe ourselves!
We're always digging holes for each other,
Our heads quarrelling with our hearts.

Then be silent, foolish mind,
Let the heart speak!
It wants everything at once,
It simply wants to live!

We don't believe children,
we don't believe drunks,
Who should we believe then?
My verses don't deceive!
Or perhaps they do – but only me!

The dream incarnated in a body

He walked along the deserted road,
Remembering her childlike look.
How quickly his legs bore him away,
As if they want to save him.

He fell in love with her forever,
With all he saw in her, just like that,
Setting his heart free,
Unclenching a merciless fist.

She was standing in a blue dress,
Waving her hand after him,
He died from her embrace,
Bidding farewell to a life of emptiness.

In an instant, life changed to death
And he experienced death's sweetness,
She was his universe,
He gasped and began to suffocate.

His dream, incarnated in a body,
Fearing cruel ridicule.
Fate, had fun, amused itself
And we are only pawns in her game!

He walked along the deserted road,
Hurrying to grasp happiness.
His legs did not hurry,
So as not to suddenly overtake joy.

12:00
23:30

She was his universe,
A plain and simple girl.
Fleeing from a mundane life
He fell captive to love!

She did not appreciate him,
Being young and faithless,
She didn't drive him away,
But she did not cry "Wait!"

She played with life like a doll,
Changing the plot many times.
She got away with everything
Through the beauty of her eyes.

He walked along the deserted road,
He wasn't in a hurry; he didn't run,
He, like everyone else, was lonely,
Routinely killing time.

A spider that spins webs,
Does not notice life's terrors,
But people all need a routine,
So as not to be burned by their own hands.

He was angry, he cursed,
Love drove him to hatred,
But he humbled himself and confessed,
Not discarding his dream.

He walked along the deserted road,
The sun was shining, the snow falling,
He said good-bye to her calmly,
And kept her forever.

I'm blind

I'm blind, my eyes can't see,
They can't tell day from night.
I'm blind; people don't hate the blind,
They take pity; they want to help!

I'm blind, without fear or doubt,
Tell me what there is to fear.
I sometimes pity the sighted,
They have lost the eyes of the soul!

They do not see life, do not see dreams,
Enslaved to worldly vanity.
I'm blind; people don't hate the blind,
They feed them the sweet honey of lies!

I'm blind! I hear people
Loudly running, going nowhere.
They live in anticipation of what will be,
And don't appreciate what is!

I'm blind! I can sense,
Nature in all its bright colours.

I'm blind and at times I pity,
The sighted who have so little time!

They don't hear and don't know,
The breath of the music of love!
I'm blind! But when I dream,
I see to the ends of the earth!

But when I'm closer to God,
I stroke the heavens with my palm.
I forget about the worry
That destroys faith in miracles!

I forget about grievances,
About envy and vanity.
I don't need eyes, just the strength
To help someone whose life is in trouble!

I'm blind! As blind as other people,
As every mortal on earth.
It's better if together we try
To see light in the dark!

Each of us has their own destination

Train, rails, track.
You can't hear the beating of hearts.
There are so many different hearts,
Each of us has their own destination.
The train takes its time,
There's no need to rush,
There'll be time to pray,
There'll be time to sin.
The dark tunnel of despair
Replaces the light of the sun,
The train chooses its own path,
We've no right to change it.
The train, like life, is cruel,
Its route is laid out.
Every soul is alone,
Although it brought us all together.
We're all travelling in anticipation,
But in anticipation of what?
Reason clouds awareness,
But it's not given to us to know this.
Train, wait, listen
To people's pain, to their tears,
But it has no time to take heed,
It replaces us by the hour.
Here's the station coming into view -
Our journey is over,
And the train, like life, rushes on
Having stopped to pick up new hearts.

You went far away

You went far away, without telling me where.
You went far away, I can't follow you there.
An empty window, darkness and cold!
You knew me for ages; you should have been bold!
You went far away, how then, was it true
That I could fall so madly for you?
Shield yourself from bullets that whizz and hiss,
Their fire's as dangerous as my kiss!
Keep yourself safe, through long years apart
And return to awaken the dawn in my heart!

Belonging to no one forever

Lamps gleam along the dark street,
Lamps like stars in the sky!
And what do they dream about at night?
Maybe they dream of love?
The lamps are silent, motionless,
Watching shadows, hand-in-hand, pass by
Along a narrow path.
The lamps burn in anguish for them.
They hear the knocking of lovers' hearts,
Over a love unknown to them.
Maybe those who do not love, but are always loved,
Are deprived by nature.
The pity is, they don't know how to love,
Or over whom to cry and suffer.
But probably, they just don't want to
Belong to anyone forever.
And at night they break the hearts
Of those who are ready to love without reserve,
Although they want to be beloved,
They are accustomed to living alone.
Loneliness is sometimes splendid,
It brings tedium, joy and longing,
And do not shed your tears in vain.
A river of wasted tears flows.
Lamps gleam along the dark street,
Passers-by will not forget their light,
For without joy hearts break,
And mine cannot be mended.

With you I fear nothing

I want to kiss you a billion times,
Life's not long enough, I know,
I want to kiss you a billion times,
Life, wait! I won't have time.

Wait, life! Wait, slow down,
You rush tirelessly, to no purpose,
I'll shatter every hourglass in the world,
I'll smash the seconds into shards.

And the seconds will disappear forever
As if they never existed,
The sun and the snow will dissolve,
The end and the beginning will melt.

With you I fear nothing,
I live in a different moment,
The stars rise higher in the sky,
I'm with you, outside of time.

I love you. Can love
Be funny, ugly, useless?
Falling in love I realized again,
That love can only be beautiful!

I love, do I do wrong?
Don't judge, I won't listen to you,
For lovers words are soundless,
For lovers trees don't breathe.

For lovers the answer isn't terrible,
And the question doesn't matter,
For lovers the truth is nonsense,
Erasing the lines of doubt.

Erasing tedium and drudgery,
The webs of fear are cut,
For lovers, our world is replaced
By a greater one in each other's eyes.

Don't seek to heal love,
You won't find a cure,
For someone who can love,
Fever's heat isn't born from pain.

Do not seek to heal love,
Nothing is better in a world of pills,
People shouldn't live without love
Like beasts in an invisible cell.

I want to kiss you a billion times,
I will; I swear I'll succeed,
Even in thought, even just once,
By loving you I shall overcome everything!

Again, I do battle with time

Again, I do battle with time
I curse the greed of the clock,
I smash seconds into fragments,
Driving minutes of anguish away!

Wait, insatiable time,
We cannot satisfy you.
You ruthlessly snatch away days,
Or you stubbornly stand still!

I don't need simple answers,
I can conquer mountains with will power!
Only I can't uncover your secret,
You managed to deceive everyone!

I'm angry with you, I'm offended,
Well, forgive this weakness of mine!
I need you infinitely,
I love you infinitely!

Maybe time is laughing at us,
Yes, of course, hurriedly laughing,
Maybe in time I'll learn its secrets,
There's nowhere to run from them!

Okay, time, I'm letting you go,
Having smashed hundreds of stone walls.
Just remember, in return I expect
The gift of changes ordained for us!

Autumn

Why are there 30 days in this month?
Maybe we're mourning the summer?
Would it be more fun for us,
If there were 31?

Someone will say, okay, forget it,
This day's not worth your sadness,
I just smile in response,
A smile, like a mask, will hide everything!

Someone will say, but what's in this day?
Maybe someone's hiding a secret from us?
I'll leave them to live in peace,
For them time does not mean anything.

I won't blame it on October,
That month will flash by.
And all that we seek to forget,
Will appear in our dreams all the same!

If there were an autumn sunset
In my life, the very last,
I would treasure it like a diamond,
Not wasting a precious second!

I would hear the beat of hearts,
Grieving for no reason.
Continuously painting pictures,
My hand would never drop the brush,

I would embrace all those dear to me,
And love all my enemies,
Without doubts and empty fears,
I'd forgive all world's grievances!

I would hug you till it hurt!
Not for a moment letting go,
If I had only one day,
That would be enough for me!

Wait, moth

Wait, moth, stop!
What are you straining towards - the light?
Wait, moth, turn back!
It'll burn you to dust before dawn.

Your wings are like velvet, like silk,
Who will notice, appreciate, love you?
Moth, light is cunning, like life.
Life gives birth to us; life kills us!

Wait, my dear moth,
You lie, saying you're not afraid of heartache,
I see how lonely you are,
As you strive to befriend the light.

You're naive my tiny friend
Your heart bears no scars of disillusion,
You don't notice hatred all around
You just stubbornly believe in love.

You think that love won't betray,
That it won't poison with the venom of deceit,
But for weak hearts, the light's
been shrouded by fog.

Yes, fog can protect us,
It hides the treacherous light,
Only those who believe there's no love in the world
Have lost the art of flying!

You fly to the warmth, moth,
Even knowing that the flame will burn
Give us your verses among the written lines,
The living can only live this way.

I'll help you all!

There was a very simple man;
His boots were all worn out,
His large wrinkled hand
Painted pictures of human destinies!

He painted pictures in bright colours
On a torn and worn out canvas
For those with painful and empty lives,
For those who were drowning in troubles!

They asked him, help us, friend,
And he could not help but help!
He even fed butterflies from his hands,
He lit stars in the sky for the night!

They asked him - help us, friend!
There's no doubt he helped people
But it didn't leave him time to dream,
He hadn't slept for ages!

The trees grew in the blue garden,
Pomegranates, apples and oranges,
But he ceased to see beauty,
With sickness and pain all around!

He said to everyone, "I'll help you all!"
He didn't notice the glow of the moon!
The trees grew in the blue garden,
And tearful requests sprouted like twigs!

The more people he helped in their grief,
The more they asked him for help!
You could see the tiredness in his eyes,
But we did not spare him!

The crowd threw stones at him,
Called him dishonest and greedy!
The people forgot once and for all,
That he had helped them so much!

All of a sudden he began to doubt God,
The devil saw it and stroked his soul!
The devil vowed, I am a faithful friend,
He descended to hell to listen!

The trees grew in the blue garden,
Fruit rotted on the trees, full of worms.
He sank down into hell,
And on earth he has long been forgotten!

Suffering gave us the joy of God,
Without grief, we wouldn't know happines!
In fact, every mortal is alone
And insatiable for sweet dreams!

The moral is probably quite simple,
I pity those who have lost faith!
Those who, by helping, hurt themselves,
They wiped all the paint from their bright canvas!

But still I remain convinced,
That the strong won't tire of giving help,
When the soul is full of goodness,
When there is faith, faith will never die!

I miss you madly

I miss you madly,
Even though my heart yearns in vain,
I just wanted to say,
That without you I can't breathe.
You understand me without words,
The best friend I could have on this earth.
You read all my thoughts in my eyes,
You see all a wounded soul contains.
You're a dream! You're a legend! A fairy tale!
Suddenly the sun broke through,
I don't need a mask of falsehood,
With such a friend by my side!
It's in our nature to dream!
You are the dream we dream of!
Your warmth melts icebergs,
You'll teach fish to fly.
You're a dream! You and the sky and the sun!
You'll replace the dawn in my soul,
I know that my heart will beat with a smile,
When you return to me!

Baku

How many songs and poems
are dedicated to you?
It's not easy to describe your beauty.
Together, we went through thick and thin.
I'll find nothing dearer or closer than you.

Far away, sometimes, in a foreign land,
I shed a furtive tear as I remember you.
I fell in love with you, only you didn't know,
From then on, I couldn't live a day without you.

That is, I somehow learned to live at a distance,
But I could hardly call it a life.
Maybe I just got used to it; maybe I'm reconciled to it.
Falling in love many times is not for me;
I love once and for all.

The smell of the Caspian Sea, the streets of the Old City,
The summer heat, Khazri, Gilawar,
A noisy crowd of guests,
turning up without occasion...
Baku, my home town, darıxdım neyi var[1]...

[1] In Azerbaijani: I missed you so much (trans.)

I miss you

I miss you.
I miss you every passing day.
You are the best on earth,
I count the days till we meet.

I remember your smell,
Not always pleasant,
I miss you,
To me, you're incredible.

You're a bit chilly,
But sometimes excessively hot,
I miss you.
Out on the edge of the universe.

Isn't it clear now?
Clear even to a fool:
I miss you,
Morning, noon and night.
I miss Baku.
Painfully.

How did it turn out like that, my friend

How did it turn out like that, my friend,
What shattered all the naive dreams?
You picked magic forbidden flowers
From my garden!

You picked them, gave them to me,
A common enough gesture,
So that I could look at how
They wither, fade and die!

You gave me a picture,
So that I wouldn't paint,
I can't see paint in the dark,
And in the light there's so little colour!

You gave me a sea of books,
But their pages are blank,
You suddenly gave me the sun,
That burns me in the desert!

You gave me grey rain
And an umbrella as a gift,
I got soaked under it,
Your umbrella leaked!

You gave me a brick house
Without windows or doors!
I suffocated in it,
Without becoming yours!

And you'll ask me again,
Well, what should I give you?
Save your valuables,
Just let me go!

You will never burn out

Like a fire, you will never burn out,
You blaze tirelessly,
Your penetrating gaze sears flesh,
Hearts submit to your commands.
You have strength, my friend,
And you know how to use it!
The ace trumps all other cards,
You play cards made from people!
You take pity on every soul,
Saving the night from darkness!
Like us, you cannot live in the world,
But we cannot live like you!
Sometimes I think you're a witch,
But one who interprets dreams.
Casting all evil to the wind,
Opening yourself up to goodness.
To protect everyone from harm,
But do you have the right to decide
to forge a sword, out of goodness?
Making it easier for them to cut off heads.

Sometimes I think you're a witch,
But I've no right to accuse you.
You cast all evil to the wind,
To befriend the angel more closely.
And you remained in an empty place,
Neither on earth, nor in heaven!
And what makes you so sad?
And whence the glitter in your eyes!
Even if I don't understand you,
I bless my life with you!
Every night I repeat,
Thank you God, that you exist!

I fell in love

I fell in love with you, although I know,
That everything passes, leaving its dregs behind.
I play precisely by the rules,
Let them change for a moment!
I apologise to the future again,
Not wanting to mourn too soon,
I lied, saying, I would try,
Not to make him a thing of the past.
I lied to him that everything was different,
I lied to myself along with him.
Abjectly, I hid my heart from my eyes,
So that the eye of my heart couldn't be jinxed!
I'll finish my broken glass,
Wine robs us of life, stupefies.
Well, perhaps, I am quits with the devil,
He'll understand the bitterness of despair.
And he will rise from hell,
To offer me a shoulder to cry on,
My lips sense the taste of poison,
Burning under the fire of sin!
Like a flaming candle, I deliquesce,
Melting only from the desire to burn,
I need your strong hands,
In them I have no fear of death!
I fell in love with you! Who will condemn that?
Subordinating time, reason and honour!
No need to guess the future,
Believe me, the present is beyond price!

Swan

Just a shot, just a bullet,
And the swan flew up to heaven,
The dream instantly drowned,
The belief in miracles vanished.
The hunter laughed in mockery,
He laughed, hiding his pain.
The hunter relished his life,
Taking the lives of others.
Just one shot, one instant,
And pure love disappeared,
Love, which knew no doubts,
Blood is brighter on white feathers.
People have the right to shoot,
But who has the right to live?
Those who cannot speak
Are often treated unjustly!
Just one shot, the wind cries,
He lost his beloved,
The cob would give everything in the world
To the hunter, to hold his fire.

He would give him his life,
If only he would return his beloved.
How painful it is to die from loneliness,
Like a bullet, loneliness makes the chest ache.
Just a single shot - a sea of sadness,
She fell like a star.
She's gone; he will never let her die
In his heart!
Even though he cannot weep bitter tears,
The tears that heal with time.
Even though he succumbs to madness
Without the light of her dear eyes.
With one shot we'll forget everything,
Time can change everything.
But it's just a pity, that unlike swans,
People haven't the strength to love for their
whole lives.

Black Swan

Black swan, you're forever alone,
Is it possible to believe a dark,
abandoned soul?
You are alone, so graceful and severe,
So beloved and so completely alone!
Black swan, hundreds of phrases drown in the river,
Hundreds of moments of our lives
drown in the depths.
Black swan, I know,
not for the first time
Time-forgotten shadows
greeted us there!
Black swan with a soul,
as bright as the sun.
Thank you for these minutes!
Black Swan,
my day was rewarded by beauty!
For this I shall not forget you!

Vampire

The vampire only wants blood,
Not milk, nor water, nor juice,
He doesn't know anything about love,
He's not lonely in solitude.
The vampire doesn't fall asleep at night,
He doesn't even dream about sleep,
Doesn't measure age by years,
Doesn't watch films, doesn't read books.
You can't tell a vampire by sight,
But something makes you doubt,
You can't disturb him in any way
Anger him or rouse him to fight
And his modesty is so great,
And his matchless silence is louder than a
storm,
In him live both a baby and an old man,
And all the heroes in literature.
Do not offer him wine,
He will refuse politely and sternly,
Having lied to everyone that he is already full,
To be happy he needs blood, not vodka!

It's a pity you're not strong enough to love him,
If you want him, it's easier to hate,
But he forgives everyone their weaknesses
After all, you cannot offend him.
He doesn't get ill or tired,
Doesn't eat garlic, doesn't smoke, doesn't fast,
He rises in the morning before dawn,
And is never too lazy to pray!
He is handsome and loves beauty,
He even finds it in the ugly,
And he shows kindness to the most evil,
Sometimes it's not enough for them.
The vampire doesn't ask questions; people are afraid of him,
His eyes don't know the salt of tears,
And his lips cannot smile.
Yes, maybe he is too simple,
Entangled in a web of simplicity,
So earthly he touches the stars,
He doesn't notice human bustle and fuss.
The vampire only wants blood,
He smacks his lips, he thirsts for blood,
For the vampire the sun is like love,
It warms, and then mercilessly burns.

Where are you, best man in the world?

Where are you, best man in the world?
On what distant shore?
I'll sail a million seas and rivers
To wherever you are!

I'll climb the highest mountains,
I'll learn not to hate myself forever
And I'll brighten the light in my heart,
To see your silhouette all the sooner!

I'll run through green forests,
I'll pretend to be stone deaf,
So as not to hear the laughter and voices,
That prevent me from hearing yours!

I don't fear storms or thunder,
I'm not scared of the rain's bitter tears!
I'll disperse the clouds in the heavens,
For they hide your eyes from me!

If I were a bird with wings,
I'd fly up to track you down!
I'd grasp your shoulders tightly,
Not for a moment letting go!

If I swam with a shoal of fish
Among coral of blue and red,
In depths forgotten by man,
I'd meet you on the ocean bed!

At night, under the glow of the moon
Awake and waiting for you.
And in a crowd hurrying nowhere
I seek your shadow; I'll know it.

And in the morning, when dawn breaks,
I'll ask it give me the answer.
I would travel the whole wide world,
Whirling around it like the wind!

Where is he, best man in the world?
Open the door to your secret.
And the dawn will answer me, laughing:
"He's here for everyone - in their own hearts."

Give me medicine.
Give me medicine

Give me medicine for pain and anguish,
Give me medicine for the sweetness of love,
Give me medicine for sadness and doubt,
Give me medicine that will stop time.

Give me medicine for the sun and rain,
Give me medicine for smoke and fire,
Give me medicine for fear and sorrow,
Give me medicine to make everyone always forgive.

Give me medicine for the winds and the blizzard,
Give me medicine so that my hands can paint,
Give me medicine for jealousy and anger,
Give me medicine to prevent bones from breaking.

Give me medicine for reproaches and anger,
Give me medicine to believe in the Prophets.
Give me medicine for flu and angina,
Give me medicine for unaccountable sadness.

Give me medicine for a false state of affairs.
Give me medicine for a fever.
Give me medicine against the cold of winter,
Give me medicine so I'll dream more clearly.

Give me medicine, you mustn't begrudge it,
Give me medicine not to be sick anymore!
Give me medicine, for I know one thing,
The best medicine on earth - is goodness!

I won't hurt you anymore

And where did time fly so quickly,
Outside it's already winter again!
I think I've become ill with ennui,
Yes, the soul of summer has caught cold!
Roses don't bloom under the sun in the garden,
The Caspian sand doesn't sparkle!
Icy grief burns the chests
Of those who're forever alone.
Why are you cold, my heart?
How can I melt your ice?
But you don't want to get warm,
Your soul mourns with winter!
And where did time fly so quickly?
I shouted to it: "Wait!"
At six o'clock the road darkened,
In vain I stretched out my hand to the sun!
If I could reach it,
I would hide it in my hands!
And then the night would not come,
Night is witness to tears!
Forgive me, my heart,
I won't hurt you anymore!
Nowhere can I escape from you,
And no way can you understand me!

Here I am alone again

Here I am alone again,
Alone again, my fickle friend!
But the wind howls, and the moon shines,
And my mind is drunk with life!
Here I am alone again; the sun has fallen asleep,
Only I cannot sleep!
How quickly the day's happiness flew away,
And to whom should I pray now?
Here I am alone again,
Was that not what I wanted?
The sun has fallen asleep, abandoned me,
And the rainbow suddenly darkened!
The sun has fallen asleep; why should sleep
And I have fallen out again?
And did the colours flow in vain
On the canvas that I painted in daytime.
Here I am alone again,
And where is the resoluteness of courage now,
People don't like eyes that hold fear,
They can't stand those who hide without a sword!
And everyone's repelled by noisy sobs,
Grief, despair and weakness.

110

Even the angel will stand like an executioner,
Over those who invoke pity!
Or maybe the brush that drew my life,
Having painted so much colour in it,
Lied and tempted fate.
Or maybe I weaned myself from the world in vain,
Can any heart have loved everyone more!
Here I am alone again,
Do I suddenly see loneliness?
For this I blame myself
I'll pretend that I can't hear the cry of my soul!
Here I am alone again,
Why enter into conversation with sadness?
I'll leave the blank canvas by the window,
And in the morning I'll draw patterns on it!

I'm longing to talk to you

I'm longing to talk to you,
But I can't, we're apart.
And I, alas, cannot forget
All that your farewell glance told me.

All that we screamed aloud,
All that our lips squealed, fell silent.
Talking to you would be, perhaps, a sin,
We understood each other without words.

And how can I forget you now?
Will it take minutes, a day, a moment, an eternity?
I'm longing to talk to you,
In this lie my shame and my innocence.

And do you know that it's precisely now
That I'll tell you all I'd never have said,
And even if starlight fades from the sky,
You taught me to see in the dark.

And even if the rain doesn't fall, nor the light
give out heat,
And even if I lack silence today,
Tonight there is nothing dearer than you,
Unable to find you, I lost you.

But there are poems, they always live on.
They can't keep quiet; they do not lie.
And to you, I believe they'll declare,
What I dared not say when I left.

I fell in love with you

I fell in love with you at first sight -
With your hair, your lips, your eyes!
I fell in love with you at first sight,
You can't fall in love any other way!

I fell in deeply in love,
But why? It's futile to ask...
I fell in love with you at first sight,
You can't fall in love any other way!

Whether you're silent or shouting - I can't hear,
I hear nothing but song from your lips.
I hate my other self,
The one who claimed: "I only love once!"

Yes, of course, I've been in love before...
Does it matter?
I fell in love and my grief dissolved,
I'm now like the sun in eclipse!

Cry if you want to, and I'll cry with you,
Laugh if you want to, but only with me!
I relished the nectar of love,
As the moon savours the darkness!

Your hands, your beautiful hands,
Are there more lovely hands on this earth?
Your hands, a remedy for ennui,
Your figure's become an icon!

Now I pray to God for only one thing,
To keep you close, not to lose you!
Yes, love invokes fears,
But I need it in order to breathe!

I fell in love with you, you know...
Maybe you do, but you don't know how much!
Having revived me, you're killing me now,
But with you, even death loses its power!

Let me die on your knees,
It's the only way I want to die!
I'll write in my blood on the walls,
For you to read when I'm gone!

I fell in love with you at first sight,
I was blinded for the rest of my life!
Live without me, if you must,
Just come back in the next life!

■

Your soul is poetry and the power of words,
The words of poems that life gave us!
You will live for thousands of centuries,
Even though you were twenty six when you died.[1]

And what is that in your hand,
What work of genius did it create?
Not only those on the heights,
But also in the depths,
Understand what is truly beautiful!

To understand, to conceive hatred from love!
Only we dare not hate God!
Through the clouds you cannot see
Feelings of envy and bitter lies!

And what is it in your words,
That makes even a rusty heart start to beat?
Two feelings are given to us in life - love and fear,
But he who loves is not afraid!

[1] A reference to the poet Mikhail Lermontov, killed in a duel in 1841 by his former friend Nikolai Martynov. It is said that before the duel Lermontov announced he would shoot into the air.

You killed in ruthless battles,
But you wouldn't fire at your enemy's brow.
Your soul saw fear in his eyes.
In your eyes, love was victorious!

And you didn't shoot at your friend in a duel,
It's so hard to tell foe from friend!
You pitied your foes for their weaknesses,
Forgiving them for their insignificance, and
your friends too.

And then a blow from a weak hand
You can't resurrect the dead!
The fool who survived laughs,
But genius lives on after death!

Blue sea

Blue sea, wind and sun,
Blue sea, calm as a stone,
The heart is silent, the heart doesn't beat,
The heart wants to remain alone.

The mind is sad, the mind is sick,
How many shadows swirl around,
The heart blames, the heart mourns,
I'm alone once again in a crowd.

Why am I suddenly sad?
Well, is grief to be restrained?
The wind's not a friend, he broke his promise,
To always keep me entertained.

No, he was not constant
But constancy in life is hard to find.
Then I had better get drunk,
And seek answers in red wine.

How many answers, how many clues,
Happy is he who doesn't keep asking,
The devil insisted I come for a visit,
Having tasted grief, his poison seems tempting.

Wind carry me over the clouds,
Wind carry me over the clouds,
Wind hold me, do not leave,
Wind be silent; empty words can't tell
Where heaven lies and where lies hell.

I falsely imagined myself all powerful,
But I just can't catch hold of time,
I greedily clutch at the sky, at the clouds,
Time doesn't want to be mine.

I greedily clutch at spring and autumn,
You can't tuck them away in your purse,
I seldom pray, but God won't abandon me,
God forgives all – even those who lie and curse.

Blue sea, wind and sun,
Blue sea, waves and foam,
My heart cries, wildly beating,
My heart's afraid to be alone.

Do not pluck the flower, I beg you

Do not pluck the flower, I beg you
With voracious hands!
It will present you with hundreds of verses,
Decorate your life with petals.
Do not pluck the flower, I beg you!
Let fate itself decide,
How many roads will be travelled,
Only the brave will win!

Why are we running then?
Are we afraid of loneliness?
We ourselves strive to lose
That which we hold most dear!

So we're not afraid of anything,
Fear's no help to miracles!
Since childhood, God has given us all
The right to choose!
Do not pluck the flower, I beg you,
It will wither in your vase.
The mind does not guard the heart,
The heart guards the mind!

She showed me the angels above us

I saw them that day for the first time,
I found out what my heart had always known,
They watch over us everywhere!
The devil wept bitter tears,
Revenge burned in his soul like a flame!
He set hundreds of traps for us,
To be his friend is undoubtedly an honour!
He invites souls to stay with him forever,
Filling a glass with red wine,
The intoxicating scent of cruel anger,
Laughing at the victory of Satan!
The intoxicating scent of cruel anger,
Which gives strength for a moment,
Envy breaks bones into fragments,
And only the weak will fail to understand!
We are all weak; we are fluff and dust,
But the whole universe is contained within us!
And the people within the universe –
are only halves,
Every irrevocable hour is priceless!
Every moment, breath, thought is priceless,
Every question has its answer!
A baby is the strongest, the purest,
It can see the invisible light!
She showed me the angels above us,
Pointing with her tiny hand,
No, Satan, I haven't lost my faith!
Now it is always, always with me!

■

Open a window onto a world without envy or anger,
Having broken the glass stained with mould.
You'll see what was forgotten in the past,
You'll notice what was hidden long ago!
In childhood we're able to see in bright colours,
The world is fragmented, like a puzzle, into pieces,
And as we age, we grow used to hating,
Sating our hunger with human grief.

Open the window, the butterflies fly out there
Countless colours on their wings,
You'll discover all that adults do not know,
They forgot how in childhood they thirsted to fly.
Why, tell us, do we see the world in dark colours,
Furiously trying to paint everything black?
There are heroes, but maybe only in fairy tales,
They do not have time to judge others!

And lips pour out miserable, empty gossip
To the heavens,
Open the window; let the sea waves wash away
All envy, stupidity, emptiness and grief!

Believe me I do not judge those who pass by,
Although spite seems sometimes sweet,
Why judge others, making ourselves like them?
While in childhood it was easy to befriend
everyone!

Open the window! You'll hear the summer wind,
That flies into the distance,
And maybe the sky will answer the question,
Colouring dreams and sadness blue!
I do not judge! I try not to judge,
Although the demon of spite climbs
into everyone's heart,
Hope will help me close the door to it,
Having opened a transparent window
onto the world!

You are my love, the best in the world,
The world sent you for a reason!
I asked God to answer my question,
And then an angel handed me a gift!

A radiant smile like the sun,
Eyes I can read for hours!
I awoke from a heavenly tale,
Falling to earth, so that I could hug you!

You are my remedy for anguish and boredom,
Joy of the morning, light of the night,
I cover your hands with kisses,
There is no one dearer than you!

You're not like other people,
The angel often visited you.
I hide my sacred, unforgettable dreams,
So the dawn won't snatch them away!

You are my love, you knew it!
I understood from the first moment,
That having seen you, I'd never lose you,
I carried you deep in my heart!

And now you are near, is it pouring with rain,
Is there thunder and a hurricane?
In this radiant life God built a bridge,
So that those who believe in dreams can meet!

A peasant was walking, wearing a watch
Of gold and steel,
He was afraid to shake hands,
In case the watch fell off!

It had the most complex, expensive
And unique mechanism,
But it was hard to move his hand,
The watch weighed it down!

There is only one person in the world
Who has such a watch – it is I!
He proudly scratched his moustache,
Puffing up his "I"!

Yes, only, I, I, I
Wear such a watch!
With it I am king and lord,
But my soul is full of fear!

And then coming towards him
He met an ant!
The ant laughs: "Don't rush,
Spare a thought!
I know how easy it is for you.
To trample me in an instant,
But I'll tell you something,
That fools don't understand!

Your watch is splendid, yes,
It has a complex mechanism,
But you can never compare
My life to it, dear sir!

Kill me, forget about paradise,
Or spare me if you like!
But still I tell you, in farewell,
My mechanism is more complex!"

You are treacherous, soul,
Your insatiable consciousness
Melts time. Unhurriedly
You burn life like a flame!

Are you a witch or a fairy?
I don't yet know myself,
I've suffered with you all my life,
Either praying or cursing!

What do you want?
What, is everything not enough?
Don't torment my mind!
You're laughing! I'm tired!
You're both a gift and a punishment!
What do you want? Speak up!
You're always plaguing my heart!
You're laughing! Well, tell me,
How can I get away from you?! Witch,
witch!
It's true!
You seek only angels,
Your kiss is poison!
Stop your mockery!
Get out, get out,
But don't leave me!
You're burning in hell, confess!
Or do you taste heaven?

Wind

Wind, you're always blowing onwards,
Slowing the passage of time!
Pallid ice froze on the spot,
It froze on the spot, and, pining, it melts.
Listen, wind, I long to follow you,
Leaping over time, through the clouds,
Let me cross out all equations,
Without movement I die, my dear.
Take me with you! And why not?
Who'll say this is against the law?
I'll wave to you as I go,
Present you with an icon for consolation.
Don't wait for me on the beach,
Don't hide behind the flotsam!
I can't live a life of captivity,
I run from loneliness at night!
I'm dust and ashes, but I'm still I!
And our names are the dearest things we own!
How tiny is the earth within the galaxy,
But nobody can destroy it!
I would wave to you from the stars,
And order the sun to smile!
But wind, no, wait, leave me!
I wouldn't exchange my life for anything!

Tell me a few words about yourself,
Everything about you fascinates me.
Sometimes my soul is so lonely,
But loneliness is honest with me!

Don't comfort me! Everything will pass!
I'll wash down grief and bad weather with wine,
Wine will dissolve grief like melting ice,
But grief remains grief when it turns to water!

Don't comfort me, I'm not afraid,
And pride in consolation is no friend!
In silence, I'll turn to God, loudly
Pleading that we don't lose each other!

Tell me a few words about yourself,
I hear your voice day and night.
Your eyes are most precious to me,
I see myself in them, as in a mirror!

O demon, how far distant you are from me now,
Don't knock at my door, you fool, don't!
I did not believe you, but believe me,
I won't cross the border of hell with you!
I believed you, yes, perhaps,
In this life every mortal believes in you,
But it's so easy for God to forgive the sins,
Of those who sincerely repent them!
You offered me sweet wine,
So that my head would spin,
And embracing my body, Satan,
Crept into my soul like a snake
In order to wound it with a blade,
It was entangled in a black web,
I'm not the only person in the world you lied to,
But now your lies have no power over me, my wily friend!
And erase my name from the list,
My forbidden dreams don't lie to me,
When they tell me at night that the angels are near.

■

When the sun leaves you at night,
And the moon hides behind the clouds,
You'll hear grief bursting into your soul again,
You'll believe that you're the only one in the world!
When friends forget your birthday,
And enemies' hatred cools,
Do not read poems aloud,
He will hear you without words!
When everything past is carried away by the wind,
Erasing the lived moment from the memory!
The snow melts, answering spring with tears,
Do not look for comfort from others!
Even if you're alone on this tiny planet,
On twisting dead end roads,
Even if you're alone, all alone in the world,
Don't be afraid, because God is near!

Since childhood the habit of hope,
Has lived in us, with wide and innocent eyes,
And we won't find a better remedy,
When a stone presses on the heart!

Whoever says there's no hope,
Doesn't truly believe his own words,
Without hope we are barefoot and naked,
Freezing with cold, and the shame of grief!

Without it we can't go anywhere,
Every leaf frightens us, every bush!
Hope lives in the bravest,
But also in the pitiful coward!

I will share my hope with you,
Hope, like the sun, dries up tears,
Even if everything remains as before,
Paint your lips with the deception of hope!

Forgive me for everything that happened,
There's one other choice: not to forgive!
We'll pretend that everything's forgotten,
We'll heal our wounds with hope!

Forgive me for everything that happened,
Or maybe it's better not to forgive?
And if happiness again becomes a lie,
We'll run and call hope to the rescue!

I fell in love with you and thought,
You won't betray me; you won't leave!
I created an image of you in my heart,
The like of which you'd never understand!

I loved her madly,
With her I didn't fear madness!
And you looked on indifferently,
Maybe you even laughed!
You have everything in life,
You were even given tears, laughter!
Not you, but she was a whole universe,
She was better than everyone else!

I could cry with her like a baby,
And the lion by her side was brave,
I didn't think to hide my love,
And I gave her my heart!
Now it lies on the shelf,
Between bags, brooches and lipsticks,
Push your needles into it,
I'm not asking to have my heart back!
Keep it somewhere near you,
I don't need it; I won't miss it!
You just have something, maybe a look,
That reminds me of her!

■

Time stole time from me,
Everyone knows it's wrong to steal,
But all are silent, perhaps in vain,
But who here has the right to tell him?

Perhaps I won't quarrel with him,
It is useless to argue with him, however,
Time was stolen, given to a stranger,
But they say that stealing from others is a sin!

And for our sins they promise hell,
But time has no need to pray,
And fixes his insolent gaze on me,
That gaze that does not even fear hell.

Time is laughing at me with all his might,
And I hear his laughter ringing in my ears!
And is that why I don't like the dawn?
And is that why I hate the sunset?

But I know your wiles, time
You taught me the crazy laws of your science!
It's not the gravity of our tiny earth
That pulls us down, but the weight
of universal apathy!

You're so beautiful

You're so beautiful,
Your eyes sparkle like diamonds!
You're so beautiful,
It is impossible to be so lovely!
Your beauty warms both body and soul
Your glance burns like a flame!
I'm lost! Now sunrise and sunset
Mean nothing without you!
Whether it's winter or autumn outside,
I cherish every season!
Fate will ask me what I need,
I wish the phone would ring!
Your voice stops the beat of my heart,
Time will silence your laughter,
Phone, why does not he call?
It's hard to breathe while waiting!
You're so beautiful, you know,
There are a million reasons why!
You see beauty in everything,
For you every mortal is beloved!
And, of course, I know the truth,
That you'll never be mine,
In my waking hours, I let you go,
But have pity, don't desert my dreams!

I engrave your every word,
In my heart, in black ink,
Night again, there's no escaping it,
Night again, I hate it!
I read your lines a hundred times,
I know them by heart!
How many stars in the sky? I don't know.
There's one, I pray to it!
What is it in you, which others never had?
What is it in you that I can't forget?
Perhaps I did not notice them,
So I could select you from among them all?
I paint your figure, yours alone
In black ink in my heart
Night again, there's no escaping it,
I smile at it, saying: "Hello"!
It's so dark; the shadows are no longer visible,
The shadows fell asleep, now I'm alone,
But I'm not hurt at all,
I lost the feeling of shame long ago!
Shame is just shame; fear just fear,
Do we need to be so reserved,
So afraid to grieve?
I lost the feeling of happiness long ago,
You managed to resurrect it!
I'll write your name forever
In black ink in my heart!
Again night, there's no escaping it,
That's why I love it!

You will fall in love with me, and then what?
Will you begin to hate me cruelly?
But I didn't think about that,
A lover is so easily hurt!
Alas, we don't remember those we offend,
Reserving our pity for ourselves!
It's easy to shatter dreams, like shards of glass,
Like shards of glass, they don't want to be put back together!

You will fall in love with me and you'll be happy,
But this joy won't last long!
Today is heaven, and tomorrow, maybe hell,
Time can quickly change!
Sunset, dawn, then sunset again!
We run through life like hamsters in a wheel!
Today is heaven, and tomorrow, maybe hell,
Our thoughts die in slavery to fear!

You will fall in love with me, there's no doubt,
Arrogance and truth are so alike!
But having chosen a ticket for an endless journey,
One which costs even more than pride,

You'll set off on your endless journey.
You're unlikely to return from it!
So it is better not to know love, to forget it,
It's easier to part from the unknown!
You will fall in love with me! Good bye, my friend!
I envy you, that you can love,
Even though we are enclosed by the circle of life,
It is so fascinating to live in it!

I can't wait for our celebration

I can't wait for our celebration,
I'm anxious, really scared!
I hid my heart under the pillow,
I threw sadness out of the window!

I lit hundreds of candles on the tree,
I've stoked up the fire!
I can't wait for our celebration,
You promised to knock at my door!

I'll prepare gifts for you,
So that you can open them at midnight!
So that you'll be the most radiant of all,
But I won't forget to shine either!

I'll prepare gifts for you,
Even if they're empty, coloured boxes!
But inside them, all those I love,
Will fill them with their dreams!

You will open them at midnight under the tree,
And everyone's wishes will come true!
And then in the silence you will ask me,
What I want from you!

I want all the stars in the sky
To shine more brightly for each soul,
And for time to hear my request,
When I beg it to slow down, please!

I want all the waves to abate,
Those that tossed my soul so roughly!
Give me a gift, maybe a cheeky one,
So that those I love can laugh!

I want the angel to forgive me,
The one who came to me at night,
And I'll ask for the main thing,
Loudly so that you hear!

I want you to always be happy
And all those who live in the world!
I can't wait for our celebration,
Come quickly, hurry up, New Year!

Three old men,
Wasted no time,
On the gilded shore.
They caught a golden fish -
Not a bad catch!

The first caught his unhappy prey
On a sharp bronze hook.
This fisherman was old and very poor,
But financially astute!
“Spare my life,” the fish begged.
I’ll reward you, old man!”
“Yes, I want a reward,
I want a pile of gold!”
His wish was fulfilled.
He became the wealthiest man in the world.
But it was too early to rejoice -
Once again the fish was caught!

The second old man hooks it,
And asks to be made a ruler.
And the fish again promises
To grant him a throne and power.

But it was too early to rejoice -
Trouble came from afar.
The golden fish was caught
In the pail of the third old man!

What do you want, old man,
I can give you anything!
In return, I beg you -
Just spare my life!

And the third old man says:
"Swim away, quickly!
Believe me, all I want
Is to spare a life!"
The fish swam without looking back,
The sea carried it far out!
"I gave gifts to them all,
But the best one was saving me."

Once, God banished us from paradise,
And how wise he was to do so!
Once we had destroyed the earth,
We'd have found the strength to destroy paradise!

Once, God banished us from paradise,
But he gave us a big treasure chest.
Simply by helping others
We shall fill it with kindness and good.

The old man put a gift inside,
It's not for us to judge him.
He didn't build a castle for himself,
But nonetheless he became rich!

It seems that my heart is covered with daisies

It seems that my heart is covered with daisies.
Yes, yes, I distinctly smell the flowers!
But, maybe, heart, you have fallen in love,
Honestly, it seems to me, that this is love!
"Yes, I fell in love," my heart will answer.
"You know you can't get away from love.
You know you can't escape from love.
You're not mistaken - this is love!"
How happy I am, my beloved heart!
And I kept thinking that you didn't know how to love!
You're radiant; I can't look at you,
You're even dearer to me!
Thank you, sun, for every morning.
You know my fate, so why are you silent?
There are no accidents, but there are miracles.
Love, you're a wonderful motif for life!
I'm sitting alone in my flat with a cup of tea,
Discussing matters with my heart!
Well, heart, go, I'm letting you go.

Love is the best thing in this world!
Don't feel guilty about me!
You won't betray me at all!
I'll always be close to you, my heart,
I'll come to the rescue if you call!
Go quickly; I see no reason to wait!
Although waiting has its charm!
It seems that we are both impatient!
I set you free from your glass cage!
You are as fragile as porcelain, sweet heart.
And as strong as steel.
But we cannot escape from love.
Let it take you to the farthest distances!
But, can you tell me whom you fell in love with?
Tell me, I beg you, why are you silent?
My heart tells me what happened,
It fell madly in love with life!

My little angel

My little angel
With a smile as broad as the earth!
I believe, I know, that you are waiting for me,
I believe, I know, you love me!
My little angel, you live in the world.

I'll tell time,
Come on, go a bit faster!
Shorten the distance a bit,
My cure for everything in the soul!
My little angel,
You're a miraculous creature!
And do you know how much I love you?
You know; you understand everything!
And I pray to God at night,
To give you everything you dream of!
And you know I'm always close to you,
I kiss your bright eyes!
My little angel with a wide smile,
My little angel from a fairy tale!

Yes, the days and weeks will fly by!
I hurry the hours along, I admit,
My little angel waits for me at night,
As the stars await the sunset!

Beauty, you are a cruel force

Beauty, you are a cruel force,
But it's not about you at all!
I beg you, on my knees
Not to contradict a wounded soul!
Why do you so stubbornly fight with the heart?
Greed will swallow you up!
But at night, when your mask is off, you grieve,
And at night you're eternally alone!

Is not your faithful heart enough
With its seam of pure and honest love?
Hunger will never fill you up,
As you blame the days for their futility!
I'll light fresh matches,
And your crazy mind will burn!
Habits will fly like ashes,
Into eyes as strong as magnets!
I'll tear my notebooks to pieces,
There's too much truth in my verses!
Every word carries the pain of resentment,
The heart dies in elegant hands!
The heart dies without colour and passion,
But there's no salvation in passion!
I'll not give more to the demon of power,
He tortured you from an early age!
Beauty, you are a cruel force,
But you have nothing to be proud of!
There's no beauty in appearance,
If there's no beautiful soul within!

■

So you want love never to end?
Let the heart race like the first time!
No fairy tale read in childhood,
Was ever written without an ending!
So you don't want winter to come?
Let the sun shine on everything all year round!
In vain you curse the cold so bitterly,
December will pass in an instant!
So you don't want your friends to grow old?
Let them laugh like children at a hundred!
In vain you curse the snowstorms,
You didn't have time to look back; they're gone!
So you don't want the dawn to fade,
You've hidden the sun away in your home!
For enemies to forgive offences,
And friends to forgive us our pride!
So you want life to continue,
Without erasing poems from your notebook?
If you want to avoid endings,
You may as well never begin!

An aborigine told me,
How a vision of his grandfather came to him.
And I thought it was nonsense,
After all, only children believe in ghosts.
I asked him: "Show me a photo,"
I really could see hands in it.
I didn't reproach him for lying,
Perhaps science has it limits?

He became a stranger in his own land,
Stuck between future and past.
They laugh politely over him now,
Today it's fashionable to be kind.
An aborigine told me,
How his ancestors were cruelly killed.
These days it's fashionable to smile at everyone,
But earlier it was fashionable to be insolent.

And I kept thinking, how ruthless
Man can be at times!
In a century he went from beast to angel,
No, beasts do not kill for fun!
And we do not change either, alas!
Although we wear smiles like clothing!
But feeling scared in the dark,

We throw off our clothes like savages!
An aborigine told me,
What the rivers and trees say to him.
And I thought to myself, why
Save him from his error?

He read doubt in my eyes
And also, to himself, he probably thought
That I was mistaken. So who is right?
Not he who believes he's the smartest.
He spoke about tigers, kangaroos,
And how crocodiles are sacred.
Now like him, I love nature.
After all, everyone loves only what he knows.
An aborigine told me
To cherish each day that we live,
About the beauty of flickering fires,
And I kept thinking about Her again.
Having exchanged our thoughts,
We said goodbye at sunset,
Now he's like a brother to me,
Time does not steal memories.
Thank you, dear friend, for everything!
Do not forget me and the green forest.
Rage is powerless and evil disarmed
Before those who are boundlessly in love with life.

Gossip takes wing

Gossip takes wing,
Rumours fly from the lips of sour old women.
The dog barks, the mouse squeaks,
Only the rhinoceros is silent.
Its face wrinkled with rage,
Tearing people to shreds,
And the glass is filled with poison,
But the rhinoceros doesn't eat; it is full.
The clock struck 12,
It was nearly morning,
Evil-tongued gossip
Cracked the tortoise's shell
Wouldn't it be better to cherish nature?
It belongs to everyone.
My heart aches,
Chilled by the winter cold.
And shutting myself in a dark room,
To hear nonsense more clearly,
I bathe in bitter poison,
Having eaten cockroaches for lunch,
We chat about something, whisper in each other's ears,
And we listen to our own squeaking,
Although it would have been much better,
To take up paint, canvas and brush.
And draw something we love,
You adorn life more beautifully,

When you dream, and don't lament!
Dream, refuse to gossip!
Dream, dreams are boundless,
They cannot be shattered by someone else's hand.
Dream, fly up to join the birds,
Laughing, they fly above sorrow.
We are undone by gossip and rumour,
Flies die in them, as in cobwebs.
But the rhinoceros was silent,
He didn't hear them, he was dreaming!

We were all taught to live as we ought.
Thank you, people, for your advice!
The humble are given rewards,
And the disobedient – a ticket.

A ticket to the other side of the world,
Where the rules are completely different,
Where the pelicans await the dawn,
And the fish are blessed with wings.

Where spiders traverse the paths
On a hundred legs.
Where flowers grow from cats' paws,
And snakes go barefoot.

Where an elephant, painted in stripes,
Waltzes with an antelope,
And the lion eats potatoes for dinner,
So as not to hurt the buffalo.

Where the kangaroo plays cards
Without trumps or jokers,
And pomegranates shine instead of stars,
Having painted brushstrokes over the sky.

We were all taught to live as we ought,
The law was written by hand.
Toads are forbidden to eat chocolate,
And crocodiles bread and caviar.

Observe the law, keep it,
But wait, wait. What for?
Don't believe in miracles; don't dream
And don't dive to the depths.

And now we wait, without knowing what for.
Afraid to step over the threshold.
We barely make it through life,
Afraid it will knock us down.

And you - take a ticket to freedom!
Don't be afraid to lose anything!
No reward is greater than nature,
And the coffin faithfully waits.

We were all taught to live as we ought,
But there is one law missing.
Those who believe in paradise don't fear hell!
For me it's all or nothing.

I can't forget your eyes!

I can't forget your eyes!
Like an ocean filled with sadness.
You alone didn't smile!
Believe me, I miss you!
Tell me what you saw in the past 8 years?
Cruelty, anger, unjust reproaches.
Who switched off the light in your heart
And erased all the pattern and colour from
your soul?
Perhaps you are sad in the evenings?
You don't know what is behind the walls of
your refuge,
There is a whole world out there and so beautiful!
Since childhood you've forgotten how to be-
lieve in miracles.

But no, in your tiny hand
Wearing a smile like clothing,
With transparent tears on your cheek,
You clench your fist in secret hope!

If you close your eyes, you'll see a warm house,
You'll hear music and laughter within,
At night you'll cover yourself with grey ice,
You held your breath from fear – now breathe!

You hardly expected birthday gifts,
The first ones were bitter deceptions.
And at night you called out in the silence,
For the succour of your mother's voice!

But you know her voice is mute,
It never answers you!
You are born in this world to be alone,
With a frozen splinter of ice in your heart!
You are born in this world to be alone,
With such sad child's eyes!
With your little hand, caress the wings
Of invisible angels who are always by your side!

Don't put me in a box

Don't put me in a box,
I don't like all this fuss.
Please take pity on my soul,
People, just give it freedom!

Don't seek to read my feelings,
My mind is not like others!
Believe me, I'm not a bit sad,
I'll calm my mind myself!

Don't cry, my dear, don't.
I will never betray you!
Don't fear the fires of hell,
For water conquers fire!

Don't cry and don't strive, out of love,
To change anything in my heart!
I fly through the sky like a bird,
On invincible wings.

Don't threaten me with cruel reprisals,
It's beyond your strength not to love me.
I won't do you any good,
Only you can forgive me everything.

Don't cry, don't pity me,
I read people's fates in their eyes!
Yes, I'll leave; I'll melt like time,
I'll not give myself to anyone!

You know I'm different, believe me,
It's just that greed gives no rest!
Let what you fervently desire,
Come alive in your dreams!

I'm different; I'm caged like a bird!
I need freedom in order to breathe!
Set me free to pray to God,
I'll fly back to you in dreams!

A man walks along the path,
And on his shoulders he carries the globe.
Hurrying, trying to outstrip our age,
He puts long minutes into his pocket.

Wait, wait, I beg you, my friend!
Have you even thought about where you're going?
Yes, in life there's a lot that glitters,
Yes, I know, you greatly cherish it.

But you're not made of stone or ice.
You're a man from ashes and clay.
Why then does your little hand
Strive to encompass whole valleys?

You grab the stars, the wind, the mountains, snow,
And the sun burns your fingers.
Do you know how old we are?
And tell me, what, at times, scares you?

Silence, he answers.
In silence, he neither grieves nor fears.
Let him live each day as though it were a century,
Let him try to live for a thousand years.

There is no time for us to greet the dawn,
But I'm happy to think otherwise.
We are given so many long years,
We are given exactly as many as we need.

Then let us step forth boldly,
Finding no cause for sadness.
Even if we are specks of dust in this world,
We are capable of conquering every peak!

How much lies on my shoulders,
Oh, if they only knew,
How many words my poems contain
About grief and sadness!
But in this life, can we
Tell our woes to a friend?
So that he would say in response: "Stand firm
In frost and fog and blizzard!"
Of course not! It's impossible!
He himself is ready to admit,
That he forgot how to smile
Because of the capricious rain!

How hard it is that roses
Draw blood with their thorns!
And if there's no love in life,
Thunder pierces the heart!

And all of us will converge as one,
Each of us has their own problems,
So much snow outside the window,
As sunshine melts the walls!

Even if there's a weight on my shoulders,
It's better that they don't know!
Even if you sleep badly at night,
It's no reason for sadness.
I only realized just now,
Or maybe a long time ago.
The only ones whose shoulders tire
Are those who bear nothing at all!

■

And what should I do if you and I
Set fire to our dreams, my unfulfilled dreams?
The blind do not fear the dark,
And it's easy for the lonely to befriend grief!

And what should I do if you and I
Tire and lose heart as we wait for a miracle?
In the sea of eternal vanity we forget,
That simply to breathe on this earth is a miracle!

You seek the truth where it doesn't exist,
Deceiving yourself, you seek deceit,
The richest is he who knows the most,
A fool with diamonds is a beggar!

And what should I do if you and I
Caught in a web of jealousy,
With wounded souls, flesh in the blood,
Invite revenge to pay a visit?

And what should I do if you and I
Can't forgive betrayal?
For help, we rush towards lies;
Lies are like opium to the deceitful!

When in darkness, the cold moon
Lights the faithful along the road to certain victory.
Cunning Satan, with a passing glance,
Will cancel out the laws of the universe in the soul!

And what should I do if you and I
Stagger and stumble over reproaches?
And, ignoring the truth of poems,
We listen to gossip, nonsense, idle talk!

And what should I do if you and I
Seek to punish greed?
Not giving food to the hungry,
Is as sinful as giving poison to the well-fed!

But don't fear the eternal void,
We'll conquer all by sincerely loving!
For I always have you in my life,
And you always have me in yours!

I beg you, don't steal priceless moments

I beg you, don't steal priceless moments,
Don't banish lonely nights!
We cannot retrieve the reflections of days,
Even though grief blinds our eyes.

The sky is a grey canvas
I'll paint it in bright colours,
In silence I will tell the glowing moon
To astound me with its tales while I sleep.
Snow burns the body to the bone,
If there's no warm blanket,
Don't ask me to be yours forever,
For us, eternity would be too short.

In your greed, time, you bring on the night
In vain, for the dawn hastens towards us,
Ruthless time wins,
And there's no weapon against it.
Don't drive February away; don't drive away the sunset
And don't drive darkness from the door,
If the rain pours or hail beats down,
Invite sorrow into the house and warm it up.
If the wind is angry, like a wild beast,
And tears the soul and fells the trees,
Do not ask me to be yours forever,
What is forever to those who love?

Sadness knocks at the door in the evening quiet,
I forgot to fasten the locks,
Come in, unexpected guest,
Visitors are never dull.

Come in, come in, I'll pour you tea,
And choose the sweetest jam.
I'm with you, sadness, you won't grow bored,
We'll have time enough for that!

Maybe tomorrow morning you'll leave,
Promising to return in the evening.
Well, if it rains in the morning,
Then you'll snuggle close to my heart!

You know, sadness, I didn't expect you,
And I'm happy to argue with you,
It's just that I poured tea for two
For I know you drop in so often!

You know, sadness, I must have been rude,
I surely drove you away,
I'm still waiting for you to take pity,
And not steal away precious time!

Maybe I should smash all the clocks?
How else can you fight time?
So, sadness, now you're here
You'd make me happy if you decided to stay!

Why do I suddenly feel so bad?

Why do I suddenly feel so bad?
What have I done?
I didn't want to offend everyone
again.
Angels don't expect
Recompense for doing good,
Angels will not
give help deceitfully.
As eyes were blinded,
So much became visible,
Only it was hard
to look into them.
Rain is falling, weeping,
The road is wet,
London isn't tired;
it roars in the silence.
What do we lose? Why?
What are we afraid to lose?
Because fear
feels so terrible.
Everyone is given the chance
To pray to the Lord,
Only we strive to lose
what is valuable.
I don't know how to cry,
No, I haven't learned,

But you can learn
In a life without end.
I really want to know
How it happened,
That I am breaking,
making hearts eternally happy!
Why are burning desires
All in vain?
They sting the soul,
burn the skin,
But there is a remedy,
Give an excuse,
Loving the truth,
people often lie.
Only we need the truth,
In a kingdom of falsehood,
Yes, we need it, we need it,
but in words.
Truth - you frighten us,
With all your cunning,
And fear
terrifies us.
Why do I feel so bad?
What have I done?
The mind knows,
but doesn't say!
Let the sun return,
Despite the sunset,
Let not a single heart
in the world ache!

■

I'm sometimes so sad I don't feel like crying.
I'm sad when I see a plane in the sky,
I'm sad when someone close mourns,
I'm sad that sadness will pass!

Yes, it'll pass, of course, for a short while
But will soon return with the dawn!
I haven't forgotten how to see meaning in life,
And it gives me so much!

People showered me with chocolates,
People showered me with affection,
I don't eat chocolate, but I'm grateful,
When it is a gift from the heart!

They gave me wilting flowers,
Dying quietly on the table,
The soul's inner chatter,
Is hard to express in words!

I sit on the balcony in silence
Writing poetry by the Caspian Sea!
Am I human or an icon?
Someone who does not know grief!

Someone who looks for the stars in the sky,
Someone who waits eternally for the moon!
I'm sometimes so sad, not even tears
Will fill the cup of emptiness!

Soon the sadness will pass, summer will come!
For now, it's a bright spring day
Let it cast a ray of brilliant light,
On the sand, so that the shade is preserved!

I saw your presence in the mirror,
You always go behind my back,
I feel the force of evil at night, in a dream
When you plunge a knife into my heart!

We said good-bye just recently!
You can neither forgive nor forget me,
Perhaps I was being treacherous
When you begged at my feet for friendship!

You are so cunning, so low, so feeble,
You span a web around my soul,
But you know, no matter how disgusting you are,
Alas, I sometimes need you!

And who are you? I'll tell you:
he, who was mistaken,
He who cannot read my mind,
Who stopped believing in miracles,
Without ceasing to wait for them at night!

You're a demon, evil, grief, a fiend from hell,
You destroy the heart from within,
But you know, sometimes I'm glad to see you,
To experience the delights of melancholy!

And in your eyes I saw
And now I can't forget,
That love didn't change to hate,
Sometimes hatred teaches us to love!

So, my friend, stay with me,
I'll give you another doomed chance,
Let us smirk over the soul's anguish,
Let pain amuse us today!

How much lies on my shoulders,
Oh, if they only knew,
How many words my poems contain
About grief and sadness!
But in this life, can we
Tell our woes to a friend?
So that he would say in response: "Stand firm
In frost and fog and blizzard!"
Of course not! It's impossible!
He himself is ready to admit,
That he forgot to smile
Because of the capricious rain!

How hard it is, that roses,
Draw blood with their thorns!
And if there is no love in life,
Thunder pierces the heart!
And all of us will converge as one,
Each of us has their own problems,
How much snow outside the window,
As sunshine melts the walls!

Even if there's a weight on my shoulders,
It's better that they do not know!
Even if you sleep badly at night,
It's no reason for sadness.
I only realized just now,
Or maybe a long time ago.
The only ones whose shoulders tire
Are those who bear nothing at all!

What kind of foe are you at times, power?
You're the same foe as a friend.
What kind of friend are you, sometimes,
power? You're the same friend as a foe!
All that is genuinely beautiful... well, you can't
live without it.
Nothing genuine is a lie, well, you can't live
without it!

Moscow freezes in the spring; the snow doesn't
melt underfoot,
May it not let me go, not let me go anywhere!
Moscow understands everything without
words, and that's why it's warm.
I still do not feel; I haven't felt anything
for a long while.

Today I fell on the ice, I slipped somehow.
I didn't lose you for a moment -
it happened just like that.
As in March, my arm didn't break, and it didn't
hurt, believe me!
I made a secret wish in my soul.
Pity me for my strength.

Moscow doesn't sleep, Moscow doesn't cry.
I'm not going to sleep either.
And maybe fear - of course, fear - makes us lie,

But what you sincerely cannot hide, you will
not lose, you will not waste.
Perhaps that's why I never learned
to sleep at night.

And cigarettes, these cigarettes! Do I need
them? What for?
When strength cracks bones,
when the day hurtles by,
Smoking, perhaps, is ugly.
And I smoke, I smoke splendidly.
Probably, for some reason I need to.
There can be no doubts about Power, manifest
intelligence and the magic of spring!

Vladimir Vysotsky, thank you
For being you, always and everywhere!
Vladimir Vysotsky, I'll say "thank you"
For all that you don't like, and I don't like either!

Thank you on this night!
And what will tomorrow bring?
Probably daytime.
Probably morning, probably night!
But there is only now, and you know how to help!

How simple just to go to YouTube,
And in a couple of minutes you're here again!
True, I had to connect to wi-fi,
I can learn to love everything you love!

Vladimir Vysotsky, you're always with me,
Let my guests quietly depart!
For I don't fear a sleepless night,
Vladimir Vysotsky, I know you're here!

Vladimir Vysotsky, thank you
Because you're alive, in a lost soul,
For the fact that you're always beside me,
everywhere,
What else do I need tonight?

Spring arrived
I woke up in the morning,
Look, it's spring outside.
I rushed to the window,
It was light outside.
I was overjoyed:
-Finally spring has come!
The sun shines brightly,
And it's so hot outside.
Petals have unfurled,
Birds have nested in the tree.
I was so happy:
-Finally spring is here!
In the afternoon, a cloud scurried towards us.
And the heat faded.
The birds hid in their nest,
I marvelled at the spring:
-Cloud, are you not ashamed?
Spring has come to us again.
And with all your strength
You drove the sun from the forest.
The cloud heard my voice,
It ran away from the sky.
The fiery sun appeared,
And shone as though at night.
I was so happy:
-Spring has returned to us!

Aliyeva Leyla 11 years old, Class 5 "E"

For now, I'll devote myself
to others, and then to myself!
Let what will be, be.
There are miracles in dreams!
Miracles are here, now, today,
in every long moment!
The weather is a radiant miracle!
So are a child and an old man!
A miracle - my phone is in pieces!
My sofa is a miracle! Electronic cigarettes!
You are a miracle!
Now I devote myself to others, and then myself,
And all that we forget is inscribed in the soul.
Only NOW have I truly seen
the people who for 20 years
I saw and touched and greeted!

But I did not look into their eyes,
so as to see them,
And do them a lot of good.
A gift was given to me – TO LOOK!
Into their eyes, clearly seeing fear,
sadness, love,
Joy, happiness, the force of goodwill
over and over!
I LOOKED into their eyes and found myself,
Having done a lot of good to them,
I could appreciate,
That in this world every single person

Is capable of giving ME HAPPINESS,
happiness for a whole century!
HAPPINESS is here now, today, 86400 seconds!
Only they call this too much happiness in life!
Happiness is in this phone as I write in it!
Happiness in the broken iPhone
that I hold in my hands,
Happiness is something that everyone
can give to anyone,
Happiness is something that everyone
can get with a FRIEND!
I'll give myself to people for now!
It's time for me to run. TRUE,
there are 6 minutes left to write down
All that has accumulated in my thoughts,
what is in them now,
How I fell in love with life, honestly,
for the first time!
Now I devote myself to others,
and then to myself!
And let what will be, be.
All I need is to complete
this poem and fly faster
Through the mountains, through time,
through life and death!
And thanks to everyone in the world
who read my verse,
To all who responded kindly,
giving strength to my hands,

And thanks to everyone who wrote
an angry comment,
I learned a lot from their words!
Not a minute in this world is wasted on trifles,
Today light illumines the heart;
tomorrow maybe darkness?
Only tomorrow it will be hard
for us to see at a distance.
Maybe happiness is infinity; maybe emptiness!
Now I give myself to people,
and then to myself!
In a wounded soul, what is meant to be, will be.
Was it in reality or in eternal sleep?
Now I devote myself to others, and then to fate!
Goodness is boundless! He who sees light at
night will understand everything!
Will understand me, but he awaits others too...
Thank you, my angel, from my heart,
thanks for everything!
Even if it won't be mine!
Even if it will never be mine,
but at 9:59 am we...
Ujugew nvcfa bkhh
Happy b day, magician Adil!

We could see angels
We are responsible for those we tamed.
Is it true? It depends.
We remember even those who we've forgotten.
Why is there gloom in my heart?

Maybe so the sun
Can shine more brightly!
All that we need, everything will return!
All that we cannot forget!

Figures, numbers! Unravel the seconds.
Unravel them, to live with more verve!
All my life I've been chasing them in boredom.
I'll have to let them go!

Let go of the load of long years
That accumulated in my locked-up heart
People, we are diamonds in a chain,
Tarnished, we have lost our sparkle.

But once we were all children,
We could see angels.
When we grew up, the years taught us
To view the world through
the mask of experience.

But it doesn't matter, it's not too late.
The clock says 12:35!
Time to eat, to think seriously,
There's time enough to be late without hurrying!

There is time; it is now, today,
In this fleeting eternal moment.
A soul without a body is not free,
In the body the cry of the heart is louder!

We are responsible for those we tamed!
Is it true or not?
It was futile to teach people not to pray,
Without catching the answer in their eyes!

The peacock has beautiful feathers!
Does he see them behind his back?
Why doesn't he trust his heart more?
Stubbornly obeying the habit of years!

The peacock has beautiful feathers!
To protect himself and his family!
Alas, he cannot see them!
Through trying to observe the law!

Does nature have its own laws?
That can't be violated by anyone!
They serve as wise icons!
Having learned to be silent and still!

Are people doing the right thing?
Destroying the blue forests!
Someone will always judge harshly!
Crossing out miracles between the written lines!

The peacock has beautiful feathers!
He is slow to display them!
But as before, the peahen still believes in them!
For her soul is more beautiful!

Angels, why did you leave me
At the most difficult moment?
Angels, you left me in the dark,
Even though the invisible light shines!

You fulfilled all my wishes,
I was eager to say thanks!
Why did you leave me then?
I swear, I swear, I'm tired of waiting!!!

The angels left me that night,
And in the morning an Angel woke me!
And past despair was forgotten,
The sun gave me new strength.

Yesterday in the moonlight
A new friend made a proposal!
It passed unnoticed as I sought,
The moon between the clouds!

Angels, you have not left me,
You just tried to teach me!
All that we crave in our madness,
We must simply, simply let go.

I'll let you all go...
I'll let everyone on this earth go,
And I'll cast myself to the winds.
I'm not detaching myself from the earth,
I am responsible for myself!

If the heart is heavier than a clod of earth,
If the paint is not washed from the brushes,
Where is the profit? Is there profit from lies,
If the truth cannot be forgotten?

I'll cast you all to the winds,
And myself, maybe, to the sky...
And let the sun shine brighter
For he was never mine!

And let the sun shine brighter!
It's hard to reach it,
Perhaps I am responsible
For the fact that he could not fly?

I'll cast you all somewhere or other!
And I don't yet know myself.
Whether I am to blame for something,
I'll lose my soul among the clouds.

I'll leave you with summer on the earth,
And only take my wings with me.
I know this isn't very brave!
But dare I live my dream?

My gift from God! My curse!
I dreamed again of a miracle!
Even if I'm not clothed in happiness!
My heart is drowning in kindness!

My gift from God! My curse!
I don't know how I can live with you?
Holding the whole world in your embrace!
And loving a Friend without despair!

My gift from God! My curse!
At 6:18 it's hard to fall asleep!
And let the soul soar; we have no idea
About the one who left us for a little while!

Perhaps somewhere mothers cry bitterly!
And tears of hail batter the soul!
But Kapila's[1] mother fell sick at night!
And the miracle again appeared in a dream!

My gift from God! My curse!
Everyone can pray, an eternal moment!
And I know that they'll find
understanding in words!
A baby, a tiger, a butterfly, an old man!

---

[1] A reference to Lord Kapila of India and his mother Devahudi. Kapila was a Vedic sage, thought to have lived in the 6th to 7th centuries BCE. His teachings developed when Devahudi asked him how to overcome ignorance and attain enlightenment

And adults will find understanding in words!
Though they won't grow tired of judging!
My gift from God! My curse!
Thank you Friend, you taught me to fly!

My gift from God! My curse!
And my heart pumps pain into my blood!
I smile again without being embraced!
Revived by immortal love!

Friend!
Everyone sees what they want to see.
That's how it is, alas!
We learned to hate the years...
There's space enough on earth! There's room!

Is there a place in Paradise, I don't know,
I've not been there yet. Not yet!
I won't reach it, I'm limping -
True, my leg is in perfect order.

Wings are always crushing doubts.
By my side is the Angel who teaches us to fly.
Only people don't notice the stars,
Grownups won't reach the heavens!

It is so easy to get lost on earth,
To fly away, acquiring peace!
Is all my truth serious?
Where is the border between reality and dreams?

Does it matter?
Perhaps not. Perhaps yes!
Sometimes the bitterness of torture,
Is sweeter than emptiness, emptiness!

Is torture more pleasant?
That's my question; I'm waiting for the answer.
Miracles have drowned doubts.
Maybe "Yes"! But it can't be "No"!

Time has now become my friend,
Everything is OK, everything is OK!
Because, preserved in my soul, there's a place
For People that is broader than the earth!!!

Breathe deeply and broaden your gaze.
There are no limits! There are no limits!
People are specks of dust in the cosmos!
Or perhaps they are
Larger than the planets! Larger than the planets!

Breathe deeply and take more walks!
Who understands? Yes, everyone knows
That exercise is very good for the health!
Flying too! Flying in dreams!

But when taking a healthy walk in the park,
Not forgetting to watch the clock,
Notice the gifts of miracles in the grass.
And it's easy! It's easy to do this!

Although flying... they told me, is harmful!
The pressure in aircraft fluctuates!
What nonsense! Beyond the universe
There's no time to measure pressure.

That's how we live: this is good; this is bad!
People are tired of impositions!
And I fly, though I fly badly!
Well, I gave up walking altogether!

Although again, this is not true!
I walk in the park every God-given day!
I read figures, I find gifts!
And I look at my watch when I'm not too lazy!

But now I no longer see the time!
I only see what I need!
You don't need to feel sorry! I am sorry myself
For those who have idled in prison since childhood!

Well, it's time, there are 3 minutes left!
Although possibly 5!
Well, now I'm going to annoy someone!
I deserved to be late somewhere!

I'm looking for companions for my morning walks!
But if I don't find any, it doesn't matter!
Boredom's a stranger to me now!
I'm never bored, though I'm still alive!

And London is overcast, it's the 7th, there's no sun!
But can that really bother me!
I know that it'll come back to me!
In 3 minutes, or maybe 5!

I know that it will come back to me!
In July it will shine brighter for me!
And if suddenly the sun disappears
behind the clouds,
I'll love it in April!

Traitors, is everyone in this world a traitor?
Is there anyone who does not betray at night?
Of course there is! There's God!
God and children!
For God will never cause harm!

You're all traitors, traitors in the world!
Can I allow this to be said?
Of course not, you're all people, adults, children!
Well, how can you not love children!

You're not traitors, you're all dear friends!
I say this constantly.
And even if at difficult moments
I'm sometimes mute,
I still love unselfishly!

And I know that everyone loves me too,
And because of this the world is beautiful!
And God won't ignore any request,
Only those who didn't ask forget this!

They'll forget for good;
having remembered, pretending
And killing sincerity in the soul!
Am I ashamed before the truth? I'm not!
Forgive me for the truth for God's sake!

Forgive me my human sins!
There are angels ready to help!
And if we behaved badly that night,
The night flew by in an instant!

Well, today is April 17th, there's a sun,
To shine on us!
Deaf people, alas, are dumb,
And I will love you for that!

When's your birthday?
I don't know, I don't remember when!
I don't eat cake or jam,
I don't expect anything ever!

I'm not waiting! Trust me, I don't need to wait!
Don't be ashamed to ask!
I'm waiting! And I'm just glad to ask!
How can you be ashamed to love?

When's your birthday?
There are 365 radiant days in the year!
I asked, I asked, I found out,
From a passer-by!

But in truth he was mistaken!
There can be 366 days!
Adults forgot how to count!
And to believe in the miracle of existence!

When's your birthday?
In April or in March?
And I write this poem
As always, just for him!

For the person who was born
under the summer sun!
Let the sun shine above him!
For the one who came to me in a dream last night!
For the one I love infinitely!

When's your birthday?
I wanted to congratulate you all!
And here's my birthday!
It is has just begun!

When I open my eyes!
Revived after deathly sleep!
I fly so happily in sadness!
Whether it's summer, or autumn, or spring!

When it's my birthday,
Congratulate me if you can be bothered!
Today (the 5th) is another birthday!
I was born again on this day!

Am I ashamed? No, I'm not ashamed!
What, should I be ashamed of - telling the truth?
Don't be ashamed, my friends! You can't see,
What is normal and what is good.

I feel somehow sad for your shame and your fear.
Yes, we are people, I understand...
When they grow up, every adult will forget,
That God once adorned their heart.

Before, my heart was empty.
Empty, perhaps all my life,
But towards autumn it came to know enjoy-
ment
And people are in such a rush to amuse themselves!

Don't cry! I won't either.
Or cry, it doesn't matter.
I'll never forget my friends,
He says "Hello!" to me in a dream.

I greet him with the reply;
Yes, that's how we live under the sun.
But do I miss you? Yes, I miss you.
All the same, we'll find my book!

I searched for it for fifteen days,
Or three, or two, or six.
I couldn't lose it!
No, of course, it is somewhere around!

There are poems about a cat and a bird.
Believe me, Jacques wrote brilliantly!
Let me dream about the book at night.
"You've had enough sleep!" someone said in the morning.

But still I can't sleep, I'm busy, I know this,
I'm not ashamed, I'm not sad and I'm not angry!
But do I miss you? Yes, I miss you,
And from longing I revel in goodness.

Am I ashamed? No, of course, I'm not ashamed!
Children don't have shame either.
Even when hurt or cross,
Only the truth is eternally true!

The cats caught a mouse,
To tear it to pieces!
It's still breathing,
In order to say thank you!

For tender care,
For sweet love,
And it's always waiting for someone,
As long as the blood flows!

The cats caught a mouse,
And what do they want?
It was looking for a book
About a bird and a cat!

But it wasn't given time!
They won't give it time,
They'll torment it a while,
And then eat it!

So eat it quickly!
It's painful to live in torment,
Give someone jam,
Give someone love!

But the mouse isn't jam!
But the mouse isn't love!
She only needs a poem
And little books!

But these cats
Won't leave it in peace!
Nature is nature,
And cats eat mice!

Do tigers eat cats?
Of course not, no!
They play games with them,
While the light flickers!

And if it goes out,
Let's light it again!
There are many points of view,
Only angels can fly

And not people.
We learn to walk,
As we're destined to do!
Let me love!

The cats caught a mouse,
And tormented it for a while!
But in the end
The mouse found its book!

I'm flying away, goodbye friend! Farewell!
Farewell, or let's say 'till we meet again!'
Or give me silence again,
This is the best gift of love!

I fly in the sky like a bird,
And birds live on the earth too!
And I dream again, of the truth,
But do you really need that truth?

I don't know, I can't guess!
I can't predict fate.
But I'm so lovesick over you,
I learned to fly on the ground!

People, people, why don't I hear you?
This may be complete selfishness,
But I can see their shadows from afar,
And for that I stopped loving life!

No, of course, I love life,
No, I'm just a little tired,
I'm flying away, my friend, flying away,
Only don't forget my shadow!

It's hard, yes, of course, it happens.
We all probably need it!
I'm flying away, my friend, flying away!
But I don't know where or why!

I'm flying away, my friend, flying away!
You tell me: "Fly faster!"
You spoke without hearing; I know
That someone is waiting for me on the ground.

I'll be back; I'll see the city again,
The plane will land in a moment,
And I'll hear your silence there,
And the daisy in my soul will bloom!

Well, if you forget me,
Or I forget you,
You'll remain in my soul all the same.
Always the best friend in the world!

I'm flying away, my friend, flying away!
I promise I'll be back soon.
Well, if I lose you,
I'm not afraid to lose myself!

And if I lose myself,
If you break my wings,
I'll fly to the place where I know
Life is more radiant than on this earth!

Thank you God for the gift that you gave!
Thank you for the moon that shines at night!
Thank you for the February that taught me
To love life more deeply than anything in the world!

You know, it's often very hard,
And my heart grows heavy, like a clod of earth.
I'm destined to live a hundred years of sadness,
For a moment I'll fly to the heavens like a fish!

You know, God, I'm asking you,
To forgive all my human moods,
I'm sorry that I dash impatiently
To overtake the time allotted to me!

I'm sorry that I'm sometimes quite deaf
To the words of others; to their suffering,
And give me strength! Give me strength so that
I can
Live with this heavenly subconsciousness.

You know, God, I'm all alone.
Of course, you know, God hears without words!
I live with friends, since I'm alive,
And at night I feel my heart breathing!

And I feel a human pain in my chest,
I feel the dried tears on my cheeks,
I know, God, the summer lies ahead,
But the frosts tortured me with grief!

Thank you God! You're always with me,
We forgive human weaknesses and fears,
I don't know what they whisper behind my back,
Give them joy and courage!

Courage only speaks the truth,
Give us the strength not to be ashamed, not to be afraid,
And teach people to love more,
And teach them not to be ashamed of their love.

Thank you God that on this night
You'll talk to me in parting!
In my sleep I ask you to help me,
For suffering is a precondition to joy!

God created man from clay,
He created angels from fiery heat,
I get silence again in response,
Probably I somehow blundered!

I just wanted to know if clay,
Hides in the earth from the sun,
I haven't yet learned to keep silent!
For I write poetry! I write beautifully!

God created man from clay,
And angels so that they could help people,
A moment flies by like a century!
We haven't yet learned the truth, God!

The heart has learned the truth, but not we,
Our reasoning minds prevent us!
But I hear the song of spring
And God, who doesn't abandon those in trouble!

God created man from clay,
And contemplates his gift of the heart,
He created snakes that crawl without legs
And feel the earth closer to their hearts!

He created birds to fly free in the heavens,
And he created fish, the birds of the sea!
And man, not to be a destroyer!
And people, so that they would fall in love with life!

Alas, growing up, people can't help becoming blind,
They don't hear birdsong, or the sea's chorus!
They don't hear the heart! They don't hear the heart!

God created man from clay
And the sun, the sky in 7 days,
He created forests, valleys, countless rivers
And God created everything for us!

Then tell me why is there sadness again,
Grief, war, resentment and fear?
I pity those in this world, and myself too,
For forgetting God for a single moment!

How good it is to be in enchanted nature,
Where all life breathes and sings!
How good that daisies are growing free,
As long as human hands don't pluck them!

Again we look for snails along the way,
Behind me, a bee flies,
And as before, I think of God:
He's never far from a wounded soul.

Who ripped the skin off the leopard -
To lay it on the hearth?
Why do they tell me rudely that
You don't have to love your friends forever?

They're wrong, love has no limits!
But, really, I'm also wrong.
I just didn't fully grow up
And didn't understand the truth of love.

But I'm walking at a leisurely pace,
Although with mad impatience in my heart!
It just hurts if you're not around,
I so scared of losing you!

And behind me a fly perpetually buzzes,
And a bird sings beautiful songs.
Alas, I'm deprived of the gift of hearing,
And so few people understand my gift!

A green bug crawls along my hand,
And the wind invites it back to flight!
Life gives talent to the gifted!
Talent, like a person, will kill the "bug"!

Trample and crush it! Feelings are like flies,
But the bird, as always, sings in the stillness!
What can be more scary, my friend, than apathy?
Better to be crushed by the passer-by!

I fly on an imaginary ship
And I lost myself on terra firma!
What lies ahead? I don't know, I don't know!
I don't believe in whatever wounded me while I slept.

The cuckoo piped "cuckoo" to me,
In the bushes the frog suddenly began to croak.
And what's worse; tell me,
what's more scary than apathy?
And what's stronger, what's stronger than fear?

Love, my friend, is stronger
than anything in the world!
Love, my friend, which never dies in the heart!
In the meantime, like a child I believe
That the leopard on the hearth
will spring to life again!

Imprint your finger on my heart,
I don't need anything more!
In this world, nothing happens just like that,
And that's why I feel joy in anxiety!

I thought about counting in crazy figures,
I haven't solved their secret yet.
You'll grow old, wanting to know a lot,
I'm young, and know what I need!

Perhaps everyone has their own figure
Three, eight, seven, six and nine.
And for me, only what is, has importance.
And in my verses - composition and rhyme!

Where am I hurrying to again?
Merciless time doesn't wait!
But as before, I do not fear it,
I'll be in time to reach wherever I'm meant to go!

I'll only succeed if I let go,
And without trying to drive myself mad,
I seek your shadow among millions,
Without it I'll suffocate in bliss!

I'm burning like a witch on a fire,
I fight on the ground like a wounded bird!
Come, my friend, come quickly to me,
I always dream of the truth at night!

Come to me, come to me soon,
Leap over all fears and obstacles!
I promise only to be yours,
And I swear I don't need anything else!

Leave your imprint on my heart,
Yes, I'm happy for this too, I long for it!
How can I live with a wounded soul?
I'll live! I'll live as I should!

I won't burn like a witch at a stake,
I won't fall like a bird from a branch!
I'll live! In joy and in sorrow!
But I can never survive in a cage!

Night has come, well, so what?
Is this a reason to worry?
Yes, I miss the sun; it's far away,
And I didn't meet the moon along the road!

Night has come, and so what!
Haven't we been expecting dusk since this morning?
No, bake a cake of yellow roses
And paint animals in flight!

And tell me, what is it now
That prevents you from smiling from the depths of your soul?
Open the window and door to the sky,
And sadness will melt beneath the stars!

Night has come, no cry is heard,
Or children's funny complaints,
Only a fleeting moment is heard,
A precious silence is heard!

Night has come! I'm not sad
I write silly poems, I read,
In order to leave something behind on earth,
If I lose my silhouette again!

I'll fly beyond the blue ocean,
To the virgin forest of Belovezhskaya!

It's good to pay a visit when invited,
It's hard when you're not allowed to leave!

I'll fly to Brazil, to China,
I dream of Africa and Japan!
I'll conquer every far-flung land,
True, I don't know whether I'm on earth or not!

Maybe on earth; maybe in paradise!
I often stumble against something,
Only I don't get tired of love,
Love made me stronger than iron!

I feel the beat of a human heart,
And I guard my own from hands,
Night has come and I'm sad
I'll play hide and seek tonight!

Well, at 9:00, or 9:25 in the morning
I'll write poems again by the sea!
My shoulders are greedy for your embrace,
I hug each one of them tightly!

Night has come, and all has passed,
It's been like that for a long time already!
I looked for roses, did not find them;
Nettles burned my tender hands!

Having gorged myself, I'm sick, my flesh moans,
I read poetry for comfort!
When will the night comes again?
I'll find out towards evening!

"The Bee"

The bee lay on the ground quietly dying,
As I hurried by
Pain gripped it,
I took a leaf in order to carry it more easily!

To save it from people on the road
and hide it in the grass!
But there's only one question!
In the grass there is an ant.
It will eat the bee without remorse!

How can I help the bee,
As it hides from people? How can I help it?
Alas, I don't know! Maybe just crush it!
But do I have the right to take the life of a bee?

Put it out of its misery! Kill it! Of course not,
of course not!
God gave it the right to live!
I stood by the injured bee for five minutes,
Those five minutes distracted me from grief
and longing!

I stood for five minutes, my mind
all over the place!
I came to a decision! Let everything be!
Alas, I cannot help the wounded bee,
As, alas, my friends cannot help me!

Therefore, deciding to maintain the status quo,
I'll continue to love you, despite all the rules!
And what of the bee? I don't know!
Perhaps it is no more!
I'm not idly asking you to be responsible
for another's life!

Each of us answers for ourselves!
And the wounded, alas,
Don't like faithful friends; they need strong ones!
Just as in my childhood I believed in miracles,
I believe the bee flew up to the blessed heavens!

Mika, my little prince! Prince of a fairy tale!
Tears drip from his lashes, from his sad eyes!
I love this boy forever,
With his pure soul; he has no mask!

It's good to be a child!
Questions do not trouble them!
It's a shame that we harm them by teaching!
It's a shame to see tears in their pure eyes!

Yes, Mayakovsky wrote 'What is good
and what is bad.'[1]
Children could fly around the lawn for hours
without a sigh,
But Mayakovsky said what was good
and what was bad!

What did he want to teach?
The right way to live!
They vilified him,
Taking his thoughts for nonsense!

He could not survive in this world,
It's hard to live an honest life!
He couldn't explain to adults,
What is good and what is bad!

[1] The poet Vladimir Mayakovsky (1893-1930) wrote several poems for children, including 'What is good and what is bad.'

Mika, my little prince!
Give him freedom!
So that the tears on his lashes
Turn to water in an instant!

In the sea, where there are a hundred sails,
In the sea, where there are fish from fairy tales,
How many words and reproaches
Do innocent eyes endure!

Wash your hands, don't shout,
Get dressed quickly!
But he forgot about the time,
But he didn't look at the clock!

We sit down together and draw
Balls, branches, little animals!
I pity grown up people,
They don't have enough toys!

They give each other flowers
And behave correctly!
Only it's futile to fill a glass
Of emptiness with poison!

If the table is fully laid
A single dish of food,
Like a glass of emptiness
Will hardly satisfy you!

I'd better drink wine to sober up for lessons!
To hush the sadness of absurd remarks!
Better drink water! Or give it to others!
And when we fulfil our dreams, we'll all be sated!

And fulfilling our dreams,
and revealing our desires,
Filling a glass for the soul with
the sweet nectar of Paradise,
Your heart will fill with the spring; fear and
doubts will melt away!
Mika, my golden prince!
Not everyone understands Princes!

I can hear an aeroplane in the sky.
Yes, the window is open.
Wait, don't fly off!
Or fly away but land faster!

Whoever loses - will not find.
Everything that was forgotten - is not forgotten.
A moment later the plane is no longer heard.
It disappeared among the stars in the black sky.

The night has come; has it gone?
Three in the morning; what does this mean?
As before, I am happy,
Time bounds after me!

Eyes that have endured so much
Sadness and melancholy,
Vexation and love
These mood swings!

How many words, people asking
Endless questions.
I prayed in silence
For a moment, just for silence!

I found a snake on the ground - half alive!
Hiding from words in the garden,
I sit and play with it. I so wish to help it, but
alas, I can't!
Just as the night cannot tame the obstinate.

I hear an aeroplane in the sky.
Then suddenly I hear it no more.
The cat paces back and forth,
I breathe into the pillow!

All we have now in the garden
Is quite topsy turvey.
I walk, I run, I fly,
True, I'm tired.

Of sweetly-worded questions,
Eternal expectations,
Only I know - there is one,
Who, through his silence,

Gives hundreds of stars to the sky;
Not beads, not clothes,
Just as a plane in the sky
Bestows hope upon the night!

"The Dog or the Wolf"

Who invokes pity? Dogs or wolves?
Possibly both one and the other!
Forgive the pranks in my verse!
Allusions, like needles,
Don't hurt the soul in the dark!

Although pride, hidden behind my back,
Touches my shoulders so seldom,
But knowing no discouragement,
I won't stop praying,
Even if I've lost my speech!

Without sadness and reproaches,
without discussing very important matters,
I'll listen to the prophets and those who
watched Eurovision!
And if I can, and if I have time!
I have to be in time!
In words and in this and in that, in verses,
prayers, songs,
Hearing the meaning, seeing a miracle!

Of course, I'll be in time!
And there's no place for pity
To pierce the fragile heart in the breast!
Groom or bride? Moscow or Odessa?
It's all confused; go figure!

But it is so easy to untangle t
he knot of broken hearts,
Just by the touch of a pure hand!
Of course I need a friend!
Of course I really need one!
But somehow I got used to being
friends with sorrow!

Who invokes pity, dogs or wolves?
I think, perhaps, neither!
Dogs need bones, and wolves love fir trees
And howling in gratitude to the moon!

I beg you, please do not begrudge
Pity, compassion, shame, fear, smiles
and sadness!
Forgive the pranks in my verse!
Forgive the arrogance of my words!
And if you don't forgive me, I don't care!

And if you don't forgive, but ask me all the same,
To inscribe another book as a gift,
I'll sign, of course! My pleasure!
I have no right to refuse!

My grandfather Arif is the wisest of men
He doesn't feel the weight of days; he doesn't believe in myth.
He lives in the moment, forever young,
His soul is boundless, warm and kind!

He can heal with just a smile.
He forgives everyone for their mistakes
so that he can love them more
He hears everything with his heart;
looking into eyes
He sees love and joy, he sees miracles.

The best of men, and the most simple.
This is Grandfather Arif, my dearest friend!
Like a bee, he bears a saucer of honey
to all his friends.
His great heart embraces the whole the world,

It can heal sadness and grief in an instant,
He treats vanity, forgetfulness
and anger with a cup of tea.
His astonishing eyes understand everything
In spite of weakness.
The colours of honey and love.

He doesn't ask for his photo from my album,
Because his image is in people's eyes.
The best friend in the world, a friend for a moment and for a century!
In this radiant world, each child of God
Who gives the gifts of his soul, becomes the
richest of all!

■

People are not friends with witches,
People are afraid of them!
Stomping through puddles barefoot,
We want to laugh!

Love and happiness are close at hand,
And that is sometimes sad!
The witch will terrify with a glance
And revivify!

But which do you prefer -
Laughter or tears?
While you're thinking about it,
I'll cheer you up!

People aren't friends with witches!
They're hard to get on with!
They eat snakes for dinner,
They like to drink wine!

So scary and so dangerous!
You could scream!
They drink wine and love passionately,
They do not need to drink

Human blood in order to
Put spells on people!
Although we are not friends with witches,
It's hard not to love them!

Those who had black crows
On their shoulders
Gave their crowns
To peace, not war!

Since there are no more crowns
What will you take from them?
Witches are not icons!
They won't accept lies!

Witches are not icons!
They do not keep quiet!
They fly on their broomsticks
Above rules and laws,

Witches love as powerfully,
As spiders,
As the blooming blue hoar frost!
They need love!

Only don't make friends with witches.
They're hard to get on with
It's easier to befriend those whose ears
Have been buzzing for a long time!

It is easier with those who are simpler,
Everyone complicates things!
The witch wanders in a black cloud
Somewhere far away!

And even if people don't care
To make friends with witches!
Whatever you want,
You'll get, if you ask!

From heaven, from birds, from branches
Or from friends!
It is hard for righteous people
To live their lives in cages!

It's hard and very crowded
To live in a world of slavery!
Personally, I'm more interested
In being friends with witches!

■

I didn't find consolation in verses,
I didn't find consolation in words!
I didn't find consolation in silence
Or in these eternal stupid expectations!

Down a long and endless road
I go to the virgin forests of Belovezhskaya,
I found consolation in God,
He always grants faith in miracles!

Thank you for the priceless gift!
Life is hard, although it's splendid,
And to be quite frank,
I haven't learned to appreciate it!

So many friends surround me,
And I'm glad! I'm happy
with the birches in spring,
Once again there's no one by my side,
Except myself, my most faithful friend in
heartache!

But like musicians in a solo song
There's no place here for grief.
We wander together in white light,
We wander beneath the sun and the moon!

Those who stick together are not afraid of fear!
Our dearly beloved roads!
La, la, la, la, la! La, la, la, la, la!
La, la, la, la!

Again and again, give bread to the hungry,
Give water to the sated,
much strength and faith!
And for myself I ask, I ask for the freedom
To brazenly give love to people!

What a life, what a death!
I stand one step away from Paradise.
Among friends, a shadow dances rather well,
While the soul dies of heartache.

What a life, what a death!
I have nothing to fear anymore.
I can look into people's eyes,
While smiling brightly.

Thank you for everything, friends.
From now on everyone is my friend.
But I'm alone. Yes, as always, alone
I wander, lost in the wilderness.

Give me water, give me water!
I wish to quench my thirst for life,
Under the sun, hiding from worldly bustle,
From an endless love of life.
Since childhood I've loved life so much!

But like the thorns of dead roses in a vase,
Life accidentally drew blood from my hands.
A flame of frost warms the heart,
Just don't let it burn!

My heart will warm kindred hearts,
And the shadow entertains us with its dance.
And I can't wait to find out the end
Of the fairy tale that holds me prisoner.

The end is the end. It will come then,
When I ask God for it.
Let grief summon me to a duel,
I won't shoot and I'll forgive everything.

I won't shoot, let sadness
Shoot me basely, as Lermontov was shot.
As long as I burn, burn to ashes,
A shadow dances. A silhouette is broken.

What a life, what a death!
There's not a soul near to hear, nor condemn.
It seems a shame to fly to the heavens,
When I so passionately adore living!

Thank you for the gift that God gave me,
For the fact that he loves me immeasurably!
I forgot shame and lies, those who drank.
And the sober people who are ashamed of the truth.

And how to understand who to trust?
Who will casually plunge a dagger into the back?
Turn your back, take a risk.
He whom you trust will appreciate this!

And do not stick a sword or dagger
In the back torn by the subconscious.
Thank you God for creating me,
I probably deserved it!

From the March night skies, the stars sent
A desire to sympathise and help
I learned to forgive everyone for everything,
Only it's not so easy to forgive oneself!

Thank you, God, I can do everything!
I'll step over all the mountains, all the peaks.
Even though for a long time I've been searching
For the missing half of my heart.

I found it! And now what?
My little heart was not stirred in vain.
A door opened in my breast forever.
And maybe he will open his own to me!

And if not, it doesn't matter!
I'll climb through the chink without asking.
I'm not afraid of the frost's chill.
Although my heart is cramped in my chest.

Thank you God for the gift that you gave!
Thanks to it, I shall live beautifully.
And please, give me a little more strength,
So that I can survive this miracle!

The happy hedgehog

Everyone left, I stayed,
As always, I remained alone.
The book on the table, 'The happy hedgehog,'
Happened to cheer me up.

I'm glad that the hedgehog, playing the violin,
Isn't sad; it sings its songs.
Alas, we've lost the habit of reading books!
Do those who read know more than others?

I don't read I'm afraid!
For now, I write.
I'm guilty of hurrying somewhere,
I'm also guilty of waiting...

How should I be? I don't know myself.
There's not a soul nearby who could understand.
I hug the pillow to my chest,
To sleep more soundly in its embrace.

I'm to blame, I'm guilty!
Only I'm not ashamed of my guilt,
I'm not afraid of a terrifying glare
Like that of a caged tiger of Satan.

I'm not afraid of cars, blindly passing,
I'll sing songs in dejection.
That's enough about me! Maybe
I love myself too much.

I'd better write a bit about Dasha.
Dasha is a miracle of miracles!
We did not eat porridge today,
But we went for a walk in the dense forest.

She understood everything implicitly,
She's not ashamed to ask anything,
Well, I somehow lost my shame.
Is it shameful to be loved?

Even if love sometimes destroys,
Even if it sometimes whirls you to the heavens,
I'm sorry for someone who does not know
The simplicity of the miracles we are given.

That's it, the ninth verse is written! Time to
sleep, But there's no hurry.
Even if somehow, somewhere, I made a mistake,
All the same I'm madly in love with life!

Even lonely, even cold and sad,
Everything lies in my hands.
But my heart is light and empty,
It forgot fear long ago!

At night I wish that you, my friends,
Won't be afraid, will live as you would like.
In the morning I'll read 'The happy hedgehog'
To bring happiness to the whole world!

The panther is so slender, erect as a tigress,
Strong, beautiful, dark as night!
She didn't learn to fly, so that, like a bird,
She could fly over jungles, to save herself!

She was almost, almost ready!
She opened her wings, believing in the heavens!
And we, in our desire for her, asked again:
"Hello, dear, how are you?"

Everything is fine! How could
Those dear to me be otherwise?
I believe, as you would, that it's impolite
Not to answer those who dare ask!

Like everyone, I love animals, I pity them,
I care for trees and ponds,
And let my panther not fall sick
Let her not be tended by caring
and wounded hands!

We are doing the right thing, of course,
Wishing to save someone else's life,
But still, taking pity on her, I released her
Into the place where you could not ask:

"Well, how are you? Tell me, what are your plans?"
What will you do tomorrow and yesterday? "
Better to buy yourself a hang-glider
And fly, looking down from above

On sadness and grief, human suffering!
Yes, is it right to live in an animal cage?
I'll draw her wings more firmly,
So she'll fly to the sky and not falter!

Crush my soul, break my bones
And sweetly invite me to visit!
There is something I cannot decide,
How can I live with and without you?

In the morning, a million calls,
And the gift of speech left me,
Words lost again in my chest
Through endless love!

Love for everyone, everyone in the world!
Children will understand me, of course!
And adults will understand,
And, killing, they will save!

I do not know where to run,
I lose myself; I'm lost,
And is there anyone who could understand
And teach me to lie a little!

I am human, as we all are,
And God will not overlook a hurt.
So why am I unable
To forget him, who must not be forgotten!

You must not love, your mind will say,
And the heart tells fables in the night!
And I'm tired of listening to everyone,
And this, perhaps, is my sin!

All people in this world are good,
After all, we were once all children!
Yes, once all children; the years taught us to fear!
To be ashamed, tormented and to suffer, for the mind to torture the soul!

And now I don't know what to do,
I'll go and live among the wolves,
So that together we can howl at the moon,
And I'll learn their songs!

Where can I hide my heart?
People can't have enough of delicacies!
It screams madly in my breast:
"Set me free!"

I let it go, and now the door in my breast creaks with ennui,
And sometimes it's hard to fall asleep,
But I do not want to place
It back under lock and key!

And let he who could not accept,
A valuable gift from my soul
Not cry for my love!

■

Do not judge and you will not be judged,
Do not sin and you will not sin,
It's hard for the strongest and the weakest
To live on this earth!

How fragile is my wooden heart,
But it doesn't break! It's not crushed!
There's no place for fear or evil in it,
There's only a desire to live!

With a chest breathing freely,
Living every day like a dream,
Mice will scamper through houses,
And cats will begrudge time for sleep!

Do not judge; do not whisper behind backs,
It's not hard to understand this truth
If you think that your gossip might be heard
By the one you wanted to malign!

And then you'll feel pain and shame,
You'll flush with annoyance,
And freedom of the soul can still be seen,
Even if a ring gleams on the finger!

Let everyone live their own life,
I have no right to correct others,
If you don't want to – don't read
My poems, songs and thoughts!

Whoever reads them - thank you very much!
Whoever criticises them - let it be to my face!
I made friends with bittersweet grief,
So you too, let me go!

Eve fed Adam
With an apple, telling him to "cheer up!"
My mother fed me with cares
As she poured sugar into my tea.
Do not judge and you will not be judged,
I tell myself this night!
And even if this world is inviolable,
You can live in it as though it were paradise!

What would happen in this world
without the Moon?
A descent into hell, the voice of Satan,
Yes Satan is as weak and lonely,
As a man abandoned by God!

But God never leaves!
And since God lives in my soul,
I'll come to the aid of the song of the moon,
To save her from Satan!

He whispers things unheard into the ear,
He freezes lips with sweet ice,
So as not to breathe and not tell the truth,
And the evening awaits the clear light of day!

What would happen in this world
without the Moon,
I don't know, I have nowhere to hurry to,
My heart silences Satan's voice,
It shouts out its wish to live a full life!

Thank you for everything, for everything!
Now I know that a moment is an age,
My whole universe is you – you're everything,
Not an angel, but an ordinary person!

I'll walk and walk and walk
Along the grey path.
Before sleep, shy cats
Torment the soul.

They torment the mind on an empty stomach.
And cold swallows the soul.
It just happened that way.
And who will help in times of trouble?

Who will help to find the soul
For a moment, a day, a century
And save it from madness?
Yes, everyone!

If you like, look here:
Envy and evil disappear,
And a forgotten face
Will acquire the peace of love.

Treacherous experience doesn't allow us
To live without fears in this world
A baby will always understand you
It will teach you

Shame is not ashamed for nothing,
Although we carry the answer.
Yes, family and friends are waiting.
But there's no room in the heart!
No, there is! It's quite full!
Again I'm being artful.
They all settled there long ago,
Having suddenly evicted me!

A hungry beast wanders the desert,
Ageing before its time,
Not taking its eyes off its prey for a moment,
It knows what it wants.

But fate somehow flung a wicked witch
Into that wilderness,
And on her broomstick, through the wind,
She does battle with heartache.

In the desert, by chance,
There lived other animals.
The witch will open her door to them,
She will offer the most delicious tea.

And nourish them with sweet jam
And the nectar of tenderness,
She leads them all into darkness and delusion
The witch has a treacherous gift.

In her hands a ray of light, darkness, suffering,
In her eyes fire and vanity,
And how many sincere desires
Will her passionate soul fulfil!

So that all the little animals would be full,
And their thirst for death removed,
Sins and fears forgotten,
There would remain only a desire to live.

In this desert all's confused,
There's no beginning and no end,
The clock stands in the centre,
And hearts smash it to pieces!

■

She's banishing ennui with a cigarette!
Well, should I come to hate February?
No, my love is stronger than separation!
And I don't regret the last snowfall!

Your touch burns my skin!
What have I invented again?
Come quickly in a dream! I want contact!
And I have no one to chat with!

Poets, they say, have the gift of imagination!
Only I'm still not a poet!
Why then do lies sometimes destroy doubts?
A loaded gun to the temple!

But I have no right to shoot a peerless mind!
It warms my heart at night!
I do what I want with a wilful girl,
But I won't leave her by herself!

They say it's hard to shake off loneliness!
Yes, I thought so too, but no!
I haven't lost it forever; cautiously,
At the age of 30, I gave it to a friend!

TRANSLATORS:

Anne Marie Jackson

Anne Marie Jackson is a Russian to English literary translator and editor.

Caroline Walto

Caroline Walton is an award-winning author, translator and editor. Caroline is a member of the UK Society of Authors and UK Translators Association.

Her books include: *The Besieged; The Voice of Leningrad; and Little Tenement on the Volga.*

Awards: a number of awards, including New London Writers Award for *The Voice of Leningrad.*

Leyla Aliyeva

The World Dissolves, like a Dream

Azerbaijan Translation Centre
London – 2018